ADDITIONAL PRAISE
FOR *HOLY HOLIDAYS!*

"A veritable feast for the intellect, heart, and soul. Substantial, scholarly, yet very readable, even humorous, this book delivers an incredible amount of information, and even more inspiration."

—Dianne Traflet, JD, STD, author of
Saint Edith Stein and Associate Dean
of the Immaculate Conception
Seminary School of Theology,
Seton Hall University

"Both readable and entertaining, *Holy Holidays!* uncovers facts and information that are often unknown or overlooked. It is an invaluable insight to many liturgical and festive celebrations."

—Dr. Francis Schüssler Fiorenza,
Stillman Professor of Roman Catholic
Theological Studies, Harvard Divinity School

HOLY HOLIDAYS!

THE CATHOLIC ORIGINS
OF CELEBRATION

GREG TOBIN

palgrave
macmillan

First published in 2011 by PALGRAVE MACMILLAN® in the
United States—a division of St. Martin's Press LLC, 175 Fifth
Avenue, New York, NY 10010.

Where this book is distributed in the UK, Europe and the rest of
the world, this is by Palgrave Macmillan, a division of Macmillan
Publishers Limited, registered in England, company number
785998, of Houndmills, Basingstoke, Hampshire RG21 6XS.

Palgrave Macmillan is the global academic imprint of the above
companies and has companies and representatives throughout
the world.

Palgrave® and Macmillan® are registered trademarks in the
United States, the United Kingdom, Europe and other countries.

ISBN 978-0-230-10487-7

Library of Congress Cataloging-in-Publication Data
Tobin, Greg.
    Holy holidays! : the Catholic origins of celebration / Greg
Tobin.
        p. cm.
    Includes bibliographical references and index.
    ISBN 978-0-230-10487-7
    1. Fasts and feasts—Catholic Church—History. 2. Church
calendar—History. 3. Calendar—History. I. Title.
BV43.T63   2011
263'.9—dc22
                                                          2010029683

A catalogue record of the book is available from the British
Library.

Design by Letra Libre, Inc.

First edition: March 2011

10 9 8 7 6 5 4 3 2 1

Printed in the United States of America.

*This book is dedicated to
Brian Thomsen and John Sharkey,
both now in heaven.*

CONTENTS

PREFACE

This is a holy day to the Lord our God: Do not mourn, nor
weep . . . Go, eat fat meats, and drink sweet wine, and
send portions to them that have not prepared themselves:
Because it is the holy day of the Lord, and be not sad: For
the Lord is our strength.

—Nehemiah 8:9, 10

More than four centuries ago, the Roman Catholic Church "lost" eleven days on one year's calendar. When, in 1752, the Gregorian calendar was adopted by the American colonies, it created confusion and controversy across the Atlantic. George Washington's birthday, for example, "changed" from February 11 to February 22, 1732, after the Gregorian (New System) replaced the Julian (Old System) of tracking the days of the year. Perhaps it was wise, after all, to make Presidents Day a floating Monday on the calendar!

The point is, the marking of time is and has always been of vital, visceral importance to civilization—for many reasons and with many effects. There is time for work and time for play. Virtually everyone in the world pauses periodically for rest and recreation—and celebration with neighbors and fellow citizens. This book opens a door to a more detailed exploration of these contemporary Western/Christian holidays that are observed by most of the world, whether religious or secular.

Such holidays and festivals (and even the concept of the weekend) are steeped in Catholic theology. History, much of it forgotten or ignored today, shows us the religious origins of certain days, weeks, months, and years as marked with special meaning.

Similarly, it is commonly understood that we employ the Gregorian calendar as the basis for our system of dating, but the story of when, how, and exactly why that calendar came into being at the behest of a sixteenth-century pope (through a *bulla,* or papal "bull"—the familiar name for a declaration by the pope with the force of Church law) is not as well known.

There is also a parallel system of keeping time used within the Catholic Church called the liturgical calendar, which tracks the religiously based seasons, such as Lent and Easter, the commemoration of saints' days and holy days of obligation (when Catholics are required to attend Mass), as well as assigned themes for each Sunday of the year (which informs the particular colors of the priests' vestments and appropriate church decorations).

All these concepts and themes have seeped into secular culture to some degree. So *time,* in these Catholic traditions—many of which date from the very first century A.D. (Anno Domini, or the "year of Our Lord")—has many layers of sacred meaning and application to contemporary everyday life.

It is no mystery that the word "holiday" is derived directly from the words "holy day." Yet the cultural and historical distances we in the West have traveled over two millennia have created a separation between the two concepts. It's worth stopping, therefore, to take a closer look at the religious origins of how we mark and spend time in contemporary society.

The same may be said of the role of saints and our understanding of the Christian concept of holiness as it is manifested in individuals and recognized and celebrated by the Catholic Church. In fact, the late Pope John Paul II (1978–2005) canonized (listed as a recognized saint) more men and women during his pontificate, some 425, than all popes over the previous one thousand years combined. The pontiff knew that by doing so he was changing the calendar, the way Catholics around the world view and cherish time.

In Catholic tradition, mankind exists on earth but also "between" heaven and earth—in a spiritual sense—with heaven as the source of good and the ultimate destination after earthly life has ended for the good. Catholics believe in the resurrection of the dead—something they share with the Jewish tradition. Therefore, just as the created earth is linked to heaven, the residence of God, so are worlds of the living and the dead linked.

Doctrine (i.e., "dogma," or the teachings of the Church that are accepted by all its members) informs everything about the Catholic concept of time. Beginning with the Genesis account of the creation, with its cycle of seven days, including the seventh day of rest, which became the Jewish Sabbath, the story of salvation is affirmed in Scripture. Then that Sabbath became Saturday and the day of rest. Eventually, Sunday and the weekend became a combination of both, when the working class melded with the leisure class in the modern era.

The organizing principle of this book is to break the year into its natural four seasons, then to devote each chapter to a holiday (or holiday season) or sacred theme that has become—or remains—a secular touchstone in our time.

Interwoven through the tapestry of holidays and holy days—in fact, virtually every day—is the phenomenon of saints. For Catholics, the saints serve as mediators between the human and temporal realm and the divine. Catholics do not worship saints but pray to them to intercede with heaven.

Although this book is not a history of the saints, they are inextricably a part of the calendar of the church—and many of them retain a hold on the popular imagination.

Therefore they will figure prominently in our discussion of holidays and holy days.

Saints are fully human, men and women who have lived and died on earth, often under extraordinary circumstances, such as martyrdom (dying for one's faith). Saints lived Christ-like lives and are remembered and venerated in death. Canonized saints are assigned days of commemoration, called feast days or saints' days.

For example, September 3 is the feast day of Pope Saint Gregory I, commonly called Gregory the Great, the sixth-century pontiff who gave the Church the "Gregorian chant" form of sacred music and held both Church and state together during the early dark ages. September 3 is a favorite day for the ordination of bishops, since Gregory (whose name comes from the Latin *grex,* which means "flock") is a favorite patron of bishops and other leaders.

It is difficult to overestimate the influence of the Blessed Virgin Mary in Catholic theology and devotional practices. The Rosary is a favored mode of prayer for many Catholics, and while it has in the past seemed to be most popular among "little old ladies," it is now becoming more prevalent among the younger members of the Church. Novenas—nine-day prayer cycles—to the Blessed Virgin have also remained a staple of the especially devout who seek closer communion with Mary, the mother of Jesus Christ, as a special intercessor and "friend in court." The natural human connection to motherhood also finds a unique religious and historical manifestation in her—in her many forms and under many names.

Therefore, Mary, like her son, the Savior, holds a special place in the cycle of days, weeks, and seasons in the Church calendar. In fact, there are more holy days, feasts, and commemorations of her than of Jesus Christ! Mary, more than any other saint or figure in the Church, stands in for the average person—and, in matters of faith, stands *beside* the average person before the throne of the Almighty.

Her humanity and goodness illustrate the friendly nature of holy days and the festive result of contemporary holidays: a celebration of the belief in the value of the person, however humble, who merits the opportunity to spend time—real, earthly time—in the presence of the divine.

The research and writing of this book took place over about one year, in which all the seasons, holidays, and saints' days described in these pages came to life. It is a look at the sacred nature or foundation of so many things in the world—of how we live in faith or without faith, how we cannot help but be touched by the faith tradition that is known to us today as Roman Catholicism.

A NOTE ON THE LANGUAGE AND TERMINOLOGY IN THIS BOOK

Since the subject matter under discussion here is Catholicism—a religious institution, a theological system, a historical movement—much of the language I use is derived directly from the source: Scripture (i.e., the Bible) and the teachings and writings of the Catholic Church. This represents a wide swath of published work that has increased exponentially over time. Over two millennia, a way of communicating religious concepts has evolved, and writers and Church Fathers have, not unlike lawyers, built upon precedent and followed philosophical pathways laid down before them by preceding thinkers.

By this time in its history, for example, the Catholic Church can employ the word "octave" with a high level of confidence that its members will have a clear idea of what it means: a cycle of eight days, usually following a major holy day. This book, however, is not written just for Catholics and therefore does not assume an intimate familiarity with ecclesiological language. So I have attempted to explain such terms and ideas upon their first appearance.

Likewise, some words are so familiar and have evolved in subsequent usage over such a long period that they have lost their peculiar Catholic meaning, such as "holiday" or "ordinary." If I use secularized words in their original religious applications, I will point this out at least once in my own usage.

One of the primary sources for definitions of Catholic concepts is the book known as the Catechism of the Catholic Church (abbreviated as CCC in citations). Updated by an international commission of the Church and issued in a new English-language translation in 1993, the Catechism sets forth concise explanations of complex ideas in cogent language. The Catechism is studded with references from Scripture, theological writings (e.g., from St. Augustine, St. Thomas Aquinas, and the theological pioneers known as the early Church Fathers), and official documents, including documents from the Second Vatican Council (1962–65) that updated many aspects and understandings of the Catholic faith for modern times.

This book is intended, then, to open the door to a deeper and more detailed exploration of the contemporary Western/Christian calendar used throughout most of the world in everyday secular life and business cycles. This necessarily involves some philosophical and spiritual discussion of the meaning of time itself, as well as details (some less known or more obscure than others) of holidays and festivals.

It is my hope as well that there will be, for each reader, some spiritual gain to be had by following me on this journey through time: through the hours, days, weeks, months, seasons, and years—and, yes, even octaves!—of our lives. There is more to our celebrations and commemorations of days than may meet the eye. I invite you to consider this point of view as we ask the first burning question: "Was Jesus really born on Christmas?"

PART I

WINTER

The winter season in the Northern Hemisphere means different things to different people. A beautiful automobile with a giant red ribbon perched on its hood, parked in a pristine, snow-plowed driveway is the perfect gift for the one you love—if you are a billionaire. Winter clothing has never been as colorful, beautiful, fetching, and affordable as now—if *now* is the height of the shopping season, with only so many shopping-days 'til Xmas!

Entering the winter season from a spiritual perspective, however, provides a very different, darker, perhaps colder vision. It is a season of long, harsh nights and frigid days. The animal world hibernates, and many humans do, too!

Yet hope is embedded in this season, like the star that has come to symbolize the hope for all ages, the famous Star of Bethlehem. So let us begin the journey into this sacred season with our eyes—and hearts—wide open.

CHAPTER 1

ADVENT

The season of Advent begins with the Sunday nearest to the end of November. It usually includes the Feast of the Apostle Saint Andrew (November 30) and encompasses the four Sundays preceding the Feast of the Nativity of the Lord, or Christmas, on December 25. The first Sunday of Advent may therefore be as early as November 27, which gives the season a full 28 days (or four weeks), or as late as Sunday, December 3, which means an exceptionally short season of just three weeks and a day.

For some believers, the liturgical (or Church) year begins with Advent—in the Western Christian tradition, that is. Advent follows immediately upon Christ the King Sunday, seen as the culmination of the incarnation—i.e., the human manifestation of God in Jesus of Nazareth, the humble carpenter's son who, as prophesied, rules over the kingdom of God as sovereign. But before that, he had to come into the world as a baby, naked but for swaddling clothes, laid in a more than humble crib: a manger.

From the Latin *advenio* and *adventus,* meaning "to come to" or "arrival," Advent holds special spiritual implications for Catholics as a time of preparation and joyful anticipation. The early twentieth-century version of the *Catholic Encyclopedia* contains a description that is redolent of how many Catholics, even in the post-Vatican II era, view this Church season:

> *During this time the faithful are admonished*
>
> - *To prepare themselves worthily to celebrate the anniversary of the Lord's coming into the world as the incarnate God of love,*
> - *Thus to make their souls fitting abodes for the Redeemer coming in Holy Communion through grace, and*
> - *Thereby to make themselves ready for His final coming at the end of the world*

This "admonition" jumps the gun slightly by alluding to the end of the world. But it quite solemnly expresses the deeply held feelings and high stakes involved in the anticipation of the birth of Christ, his coming to us through the sacrament of the Eucharist, or Holy Communion, and finally his return to the faithful at the end of all time.

Catholics have a lot of preparation to do for this season, and it doesn't just involve shopping and wrapping gifts.

Today, for better or worse, the weeks leading up to Christmas are heavily commercialized. We are all familiar with the count of shopping days remaining until Christmas, which can create pressures for all of us who want to participate fully in the gift-giving aspects of the season. More and more, the contemporary Church has been encouraging families to focus on the spiritual nature of these days and weeks.

Catholics prepare through fasting and prayer, much in the tradition of other religions, including Catholicism's monotheistic brethren, Judaism and Islam, as well as the great Eastern traditions, such as Buddhism. This is why Advent has commonly been known as the "little Lent." It is a substantial amount of time set apart from the rest of the calendar, imbued with a deep feeling of anticipation of a pending event that will cleanse and renew the world.

ORIGINS OF THE SEASON

So how and when did this season come into being? Like many traditions in the Church, we do not know for certain. We do, however, know that by the mid-seventh century, Advent was established in the Church of Rome because a sermon of Pope Gregory the Great, delivered for the second Sunday of Advent, survives. That gives a precedent of nearly a millennium and a half of ecclesiastical observance.

Some earlier clues include a canon, or law, in the Synod of Saragossa in 380, which prescribes that from December

17 to the Feast of the Epiphany, January 6, "no person should be permitted to absent himself from church." That is a long, potentially claustrophobic three weeks, perhaps a precursor to the mature feast of four Sundays preceding the "12 days of Christmas" that, indeed, end on January 6.

Other collections of homilies by clerics of lesser reputation than Pope Gregory I can be dated as far back as the mid-fifth or early sixth centuries, but no Church law with general application can be found on the books until very late in the sixth (then the middle of the seventh) century—starting in Gaul (modern-day France) and then Spain, which hew rather closely to the Advent period of fasting for 40 to 50 days in November and December.

In the Greek, or Eastern Orthodox Church, there are no surviving documents on the observance of Advent earlier than the eighth century. When it was established, however, it was clearly the same three-week to 50-day period of rigorous abstinence from which the Western Church eventually pulled back, one might say, to focus on the liturgical celebration rather than the hair-shirt emphasis on self-denial. There would, after all, be more of that come Lent, in late winter and spring north of the equator.

As with any major division of earthly time, the Church needs specifically religious reasons to set aside daily life practices—and even daily needs—to observe certain rituals. So the theologians—like Gregory and the other Church Fathers of the early medieval world—sought their warrants in Scripture. In particular, they looked at the very first book of the Bible as one key source. Genesis 1:31 states: *God looked at everything he had made, and he found it very good. Evening came, and morning followed—the sixth day.* And Genesis 2:2–3: *Since on the seventh day God was finished with the work he had been doing, he rested on the seventh day from all the work he had undertaken. So God blessed the seventh day and made it holy, because on it he rested from all the work he had done.* These scriptural passages seemed to call explicitly for a day set apart for rest and worship. Catholic tradition extends single days into seasons when the need for separation from "normal" time seems necessary. A once-popular notion that held currency among Catholics from the middle of the first millennium on, though with no basis other than supposition and perhaps an element of superstition, was that the four weeks of Advent were meant to symbolize the four thousand years of darkness in which the world was enveloped before the birth of Christ.

Advent remains rich in symbol, ritual, meaning, and color for Roman Catholics. Yes, it is a dark time of the year—moving inexorably toward the darkest time of all, the shortest day and longest night. But it is not wholly somber or forbidding. Especially for children who are raised in the Catholic tradition, the season holds strange and fascinating images, challenges, and promises.

Families can harness their kids' fascination with the holiday of Christmas to gain their attention for religious instruction during these late autumn and winter days.

Truly devout Catholics, in fact, lament that the full impact of Advent is too often lost in the modern world, yet another victim of the seemingly unstoppable secularization of all societies in the West. But the panoply of symbols, many based on ancient religious and natural images, are available to anyone who might want to apply them to personal devotions and spiritual practices.

The Advent wreath is one of the most common customs, observed both in the home and within the church. In Catholic parishes the Advent wreath is visible in the sanctuary throughout the pre-Christmas season as an additional decoration and as a part of the liturgy itself, marking the "countdown" to the birthday of Jesus.

As the season progresses, significant dates occur during Advent including December 6, St. Nicholas Day, and December 13, the Feast of St. Lucy. In Holland, on the eve of the former, a child will put out a shoe with the hope that the bishop and saint after whom Santa Claus is named will visit and leave behind a gift, such as a nut or a toy. The latter denotes the first day of the Christmas season in Sweden. Distinctive seasonal cakes are named after Lucy, a virgin and martyr of the early fourth century.

Wedged into the cycle that includes Advent is an important feast—that of the Blessed Virgin (known also as a "Marian" feast). In fact, it is one of the most important: December 8 is marked as a holy day of obligation (a day on which Catholics are required to attend Mass) in honor of the Immaculate Conception. Established by the Eastern Church during the eighth century as the feast day of the Conception of Saint Anne, it was adopted as a Roman Catholic feast day by Pope Sixtus IV in the fifteenth century, and then elevated to a solemnity and holy day of obligation in 1854, when Pius IX defined the doctrine of Mary being born without sin.

The "splendor of an entirely unique holiness" by which Mary is "enriched from the first instant of her conception" comes wholly from Christ: she is "redeemed, in a more exalted fashion, by reason of the merits of her Son," according to the contemporary Church (in the Vatican II document, *Lumen Gentium*). On this day the priest wears white vestments symbolizing her purity.

The contemporary Spanish custom is to treat the feast of the Immaculate Conception as Mother's Day.

ADVENT COLORS AND SYMBOLS

Priest's vestments: The vestments of the Mass throughout Advent are purple or violet—a dark bluish color representing sorrow and repentance. This pattern is broken by vesting in a rose-colored chasuble on the third Sunday of Advent only.

Advent calendar: Children learn about the season from a calendar that features doors on each day, with a treat or surprise behind the door, such as candy.

Advent wreath: This wreath, with its German origins, is the most familiar image and custom associated with Advent. Made of evergreens, lying flat, it holds four bright candles, three purple and one a pink or "rose" color emblematic of the third Sunday of the season, known as Gaudete (Joyful) Sunday. Each Sunday a new candle is lit, prayers are offered, and hymns are sung.

Jesse Tree: Jesus is said to be descended from King David, son of Jesse, and thus is a member of Jesse's family tree. Symbols, like ornaments, are hung from this symbolic tree (or representation of a tree) representing people and events from history, Old Testament and New.

Crèche (Nativity scene) with the empty manger: Technically, the crèche is not to be displayed with the baby Jesus in his manger until Christmas Day. Often the three wise men, or the Magi, are added to the scene only toward the end of the Christmas season, close to their day, January 6, the Feast of the Epiphany.

CHAPTER 2

CHRISTMAS

Christmas means "Christ's Mass" and represents, for Catholics, the first and perhaps most popular holy day on the calendar. Who doesn't love Christmas? Although it was not among the earliest festivals of the Christian Church, by the mid-fourth century, through popular practice that was then sanctioned by Church authority, December 25 was established in Rome as the "birthday" of Christ. The Son of God who had eclipsed the pagan sun god, Sol Invictus, whose birth had previously been celebrated on the same day.

Familiar names associated with Christmas are derived from various languages and cultures. For example, in Old English it is *Cristes Maesse*, in Dutch *Kerst-misse*. The Latin *Dies Natalis*, meaning "Day of Nativity," becomes the Italian *Il Natale*, and the French *Noël*.

In his writing on lunar theory, Isaac Newton (who was born on Christmas in 1642) noted the coincidence of December 25 and the winter solstice that the Roman state had marked as *Dies Natalis, Solis Invicti*, the nativity of the same "invincible" sun god. By the fourth century of the Christian era, Christmas fell nine months after the spring equinox, March 25. This also happens to be the Annunciation, when Jesus was conceived in the womb of the young Virgin Mary through the announcement by the Archangel Gabriel and her acceptance of the Holy Spirit. All very mysterious and intriguing.

Another connection with pagan worship must be mentioned—that of the cult of the god Mithras, which was popular among the Roman military men. According to Michael Molnar, "Mithras was a celestial god who was evidently seen as responsible for the precession of the equinox." In this belief system, he ruled with Sol over the cosmos, directing the movements of the stars and planets.

OBSERVANCE IN THE EARLY CHURCH

Early echoes of the Feast of the Nativity of Christ were evident as far back as A.D. 200 in Egypt. Clement of Alexandria, one of the most important leaders and theologians of the late second-century Church, wrote that certain Egyptian theologians "over curiously" assign the day of Christ's birth as May 20 in the 28th year of the reign of the Emperor Augustus (the nonexistent year A.D. "0"), which was the 25th day of the ninth month of their calendar.

Other early scholars and stargazers wanted the date to coincide with March 25, the spring equinox and the day of the creation of the sun. Clement chronicled other assignments of Christmas in popular usage, which included January 6 and January 10. It seems as though no one could decide when Christ was born. It is interesting to read through the tangled accounts of these early years, making it clear that the Church itself was nowhere near a monolithic institution, but rather an array of churches and local communities with their own deep traditions, needs, and biases in the practice of the Christian faith.

In the mists of late antiquity, the two feasts—the birthday itself and the visitation of the Magi, the three wise men or astrologers from the East—were separated, and have more or less remained so up to today.

The December 25 date of the Nativity was adopted in the late fourth century by the churches of Jerusalem, Antioch, and Constantinople—after Rome—and in Egypt around A.D. 430. The churches of the East in Cyprus, Mesopotamia, Asia Minor, and Armenia held on to the January 6 date, though the great preacher and Church Father Gregory of Nyssa advocated for the December feast in Cappadocia around 380 in a sermon on St. Stephen's Day, December 26 (arguing "backwards," as it were, from the recognition of Stephen as the closest "imitator" of the one born on the previous day).

Gregory's contemporary critics and colleagues (and fellow saints), John Chrysostom and Gregory Nazianzen, were also instrumental in fixing the December celebration in the liturgical calendar. The so-called *Chronography* of A.D. 354, published in Rome, offers the first written mixture of planetary astrology, Roman mythology, and pagan religious imagery adapted to contemporary purposes of placing Church holy days on solar dates, including the winter solstice for the birthday of Jesus and the summer solstice for the birthday of John the Baptist, Christ's cousin and precursor. In turn, the date of the conception for each was the alternate equinox.

So it can be stated with some authority that by about A.D. 400, the Church (in the West, at least) had fixed Christmas on December 25.

It has not helped the process of sorting out the conflicts around dating Christmas that the older-style Julian calendar was replaced by the more contemporary Gregorian Calendar, which differed by almost exactly the span between December 25 and January 6! To this day, in fact, the Eastern Orthodox churches celebrate the Nativity of Christ on or around the later date.

It was the formidable Christian apologist Tertullian, in the early third century, who first cast doubt on the calculation of the year of Jesus' birth by pointing out that if the Gospel account of the Roman census (held every 14 years) was correct, it is likely that he was born in either A.D. 6 or 8

B.C. The former was too late, but the latter coincided with the reigns of both Augustus (27 B.C.–A.D. 14) and Herod the Great (37–4 B.C.). The two rulers are important historical touchstones on which to base dates for other persons and events.

What about that date, then?

When all is said and done, based on centuries of speculation and research, today's historians and biblical scholars agree that December 25 is not the true "birthday" of Jesus of Nazareth, nor the year "0" Anno Domini the correct year.

If these are accepted as facts, then when was he born?

First, let's review what *happened,* as the Gospel writer Luke wrote around A.D. 90. Luke 2:1–20:

In those days a decree went out from Caesar Augustus that the whole world should be enrolled. This was the first enrollment, when Quirinius was governor of Syria. So all went to be enrolled, each to his own town. And Joseph too went up from Galilee from the town of Nazareth to Judea, to the city of David that is called Bethlehem, because he was of the house and family of David, to be enrolled with Mary, his betrothed, who was with child.

While they were there, the time came for her to have her child, and she gave birth to her firstborn son. She wrapped him in swaddling clothes and laid him in a manger, because there was no room for them in the inn.

*Now there were shepherds in that region living in the fields
and keeping the night watch over their flock. The angel of the
Lord appeared to them and the glory of the Lord shone around
them, and they were struck with great fear.*

*The angel said to them: "Do not be afraid; for behold, I pro-
claim to you good news of great joy that will be for all the people.
For today in the city of David a savior has been born for you who
is Messiah and Lord. And this will be a sign for you: you will find
the infant wrapped in swaddling clothes and lying in a manger."*

*And suddenly there was a multitude of the heavenly host
with the angel, praising God and saying: "Glory to God in the
highest and on earth peace to those on whom his favor rests."*

*When the angels went away from them to heaven, the shep-
herds said to one another, "Let us go, then, to Bethlehem to see
this thing that has taken place, which the Lord has made known
to us." So they went in haste and found Mary and Joseph, and
the infant lying in the manger.*

*When they saw this, they made known the message that had
been told them about this child. All who heard it were amazed by
what had been told them by the shepherds. And Mary kept all
these things, reflecting on them in her heart. Then the shepherds
returned, glorifying and praising God for all they had heard and
seen, just as it had been told to them.*

One of the most compelling new theories of the date of
Christ's birth is contained in a fascinating study by a former
Rutgers University astronomer, Michael R. Molnar. In 1999

Dr. Molnar published *The Star of Bethlehem: The Legacy of the Magi,* a work incorporating astronomy, astrology, and archaeology that points to a possible date of April 17, 6 B.C. as the birthday of the King of the Jews.

And how does he get to that point? The scriptural accounts of the birth of Jesus in Matthew and Luke (both derived from the earlier Gospel of Mark and other written and oral sources) contain tantalizing clues and specific references to the star present at Jesus' birth; the Magi from the East who followed the star announcing a royal birth; and the fear of King Herod (who was familiar with astrological signs) that a new king might arise to threaten his dynasty.

Again, let's look closely at the Gospel narrative for details about the events and persons involved. Here is Matthew 2:1–12:

When Jesus was born in Bethlehem of Judea, in the days of King Herod, behold, magi from the east arrived in Jerusalem, saying, "Where is the newborn king of the Jews? We saw his star at its rising and have come to do him homage."

When King Herod heard this, he was greatly troubled, and all Jerusalem with him. Assembling all the chief priests and the scribes of the people, he inquired of them where the Messiah was to be born. They said to him, "In Bethlehem of Judea, for thus it has been written through the prophet: 'And you, Bethlehem, land of Judah, are by no means the least among the rulers of Judah; since from you shall come a ruler, who is to shepherd my people Israel."

> *Then Herod called the magi secretly and ascertained from them the time of the star's appearance. He sent them to Bethlehem and said, "Go and search diligently for the child. When you have found him, bring me word, that I too may go and do him homage."*
>
> *After their audience with the king they set out. And behold, the star that they had seen at its rising preceded them, until it came and stopped over the place where the child was. They were overjoyed at seeing the star, and on entering the house they saw the child with Mary his mother. They prostrated themselves and did him homage. Then they opened their treasures and offered him gifts of gold, frankincense, and myrrh.*
>
> *And having been warned in a dream not to return to Herod, they departed for their country by another way.*

Molnar's discovery of an ancient Roman-era coin with the image of a ram looking back at a star helped to support a hypothesis that ancient astrologers had expected, then seen, a lunar eclipse of the planet Jupiter as an astrological herald of the Anointed One (a king and/or messiah of Judea). This "star" phenomenon visible in the East was chronicled in Matthew's Gospel and verified by a meticulous, computer-generated astronomical re-creation of the event. Thus Molnar writes: "Historical records show that the seemingly unimpressive planetary alignments of April 17 [6 B.C.] were exactly what astrologers such as the Magi believed to constitute portents of a royal birth."

CHRISTMAS EVE

Catholics love vigils, that is, the eve of the holy day. In fact, in German, Christmas is named after the vigil: *Weihnachtsfest,* meaning "holy night" or "night of blessing." When, after Vatican II, members of the Catholic Church were granted permission to fulfill their Sunday obligation by attending Mass on Saturday evening (the vigil of Sunday), a subset of the faithful took advantage of the new rule. In virtually any Catholic Church in the United States, you can go to a 5:00 or 5:30 P.M. liturgy on a Saturday and find a reliable core of parishioners who have made that celebration their own. They will also be there the next Saturday, and the Saturday after that, and the Saturday after that . . . often sitting in exactly the same pews (another typical Catholic ritual). This practice of attending the vigil Mass extends to most other major holy days throughout the year. And it arguably brings more people into the pews, which must make pastors and bishops happy.

Many Catholics, including those of Italian and Slavic heritages, open gifts, have elaborate dinners on Christmas Eve, and attend the "midnight" (or late night) Mass as a long-standing family tradition.

THE CHRISTMAS TREE

The Christmas tree is now a nearly universal symbol of the holiday. Its history has been well documented. "O Tannenbaum" is a hymn to the presumably German-invented custom of the Christmas tree. The tree's roots go back to pagan times when evergreens were first used to decorate houses and churches in midwinter, and in Christian symbolism the tree, an evergreen, symbolized immortality, since it was adorned with apples, which represented Adam's fall in the Garden of Eden.

Martin Luther has been credited, in legend, with the first lighted tree: inspired by the stars on a Christmas Eve, he put candles in his family's Christmas tree to inspire reverence and awe in his children for Christ as the light of the world.

The earliest mention of a Christmas tree in the United States is found in a diary entry on December 20, 1821, by Pennsylvanian Matthew Zahm: "Sally and our Thos. And Wm. Hensel was out for Christmas trees, on the hill at Kendrick's saw mill." And the first American illustration of a Christmas tree was printed in 1836 in a book titled *The Stranger's Gift: A Christmas and New Year's Present*.

Now, in the twenty-first century, the Christmas tree is the universal symbol of the season for Protestants, Catholics, and nonreligious celebrants alike.

CHRISTMAS CARDS

As Jock Elliot writes in *Inventing Christmas: How Our Holiday Came to Be*, "While Germany can claim credit for the first Christmas trees, the prize for the first Christmas card goes to England." He explains that there were many precursors of the familiar Christmas card. Egyptians exchanged gifts at the turn of the year, as did the Romans on January 1: they exchanged coins and lamps, some of which were inscribed with new year's wishes.

The introduction of printing meant a revolution in mass communication throughout Europe. By the early nineteenth century, cards were already being printed for any and all occasions—feast days, holidays, and birthdays—with greetings to be filled in by the sender.

Then, in 1843, an energetic Englishman named Henry Cole got an idea. He commissioned artist John Calcott Horsley to design the first Christmas card. At the top of the card (in the form of a triptych) is a dotted line for the name of the addressee, and at the bottom is another one for the sender's signature. One thousand cards were printed and hand colored, selling for one shilling each. Later, Cole was to be involved in the founding of the Victoria and Albert Museum, the penny post, perforated postage stamps, and postcards.

The Christmas card business exploded in volume and appeal almost immediately. Today, more than a century and a half later, 2.5 billion cards are printed annually in the United States alone (and St. Valentine's Day and Mother's Day cards also sell billions).

GIFTS

The practice of giving gifts at Christmastime comes from the story of the gifts of the Magi: gold, frankincense, and myrrh, presented to the Holy Child as recognition of his royal birth.

As noted earlier, such presents have deep roots in ancient Egypt and imperial Rome, both pagan cultures, and were easily adapted for modern consumers, welcomed by merchants and advertisers alike. Who doesn't remember making a Christmas list to be mailed to Santa Claus at the North Pole or at least to put under one's parents' noses with high hopes?

THE YULE LOG

This is another northern European custom linked to the season, now probably best known in its electronic version as a continuous TV broadcast of an image of a burning log. Yule, originally *Jul,* is the pagan Scandinavian winter festival, and the name has long since become synonymous with Christmas. For both pagans and Christians, such a burning log gives off light and heat in the dark nights of the winter solstice.

SEASONAL COLORS

The colors of the season are varied, and rich with meaning: Moving from the days of fasting and anticipation that make up the season of Advent, with dark and solemn colors that move through the increasingly dark days of the calendar, Christmas opens up the church and the home with bright lights and colors. During the Christmas Mass, the priest wears vestments of white, sometimes highlighted with gold.

The holiday also brings out the combination of red and green in decorations, gift wrappings, and ribbons. These colors derive from holly (berries and leaves) and poinsettias (flowers and leaves).

Practically everyone has a favorite memory or image of Christmastime. Films, from the various versions of *A Christmas Carol* to *It's a Wonderful Life* and *Home Alone,* offer vivid pictures and warm messages of human kindness, even admitting our deep human frailties and failings.

The Academy Award–winning film *The Lion in Winter* is set in King Henry II's castle at Chignon during a "Christmas court" at which the king gathers his family, allies, and enemies—including the beautiful, if aged, Queen Eleanor of Aquitaine. There is a Christmas tree and a patina of religious observance amid the mean environs of the cold castle among the rivalrous clan. Henry actively encourages the squabbling and plotting among his three surviving sons, each of whom seeks to succeed him on the throne of England.

"Well, what shall we hang, the holly or each other?" Henry asks ironically at one point.

There is a great scene of Eleanor wrapping gifts in charmingly coarse but colorful cloth and writing gift tags. Later she appears laden with the gifts and places them beneath the tree with the help of her husband.

Then there is the recurring image of the Christmas candle as it burns down. "When I was little Christmas was a time of great confusion to me," Eleanor tells Alais, Henry's young mistress and a pawn in the family's political machinations. Even in moments of great stress—perhaps especially in such moments—the season is present in the hearts of the protagonists.

Can it be this way for all of us? Life goes on. Christmas marks a new beginning, possibilities, hope, and even joy—despite the sins and imperfections of those who claim to follow their Lord day by day.

CHAPTER 3

NEW YEAR'S, EPIPHANY, AND PRESENTATION

C hristmas, of course, is only the beginning. We extend
this holiday season by planning vacations and family
time as the new year approaches. Many institutions
such as schools, public and private, government offices, and
companies large and small close their doors and give students
and employees a lengthy break during this period.

Time moves inexorably forward, leaving Christmas
wrapping paper and packages behind, toys already broken,
Christmas cards taped to the refrigerator door, and the limbs
of the tree sagging, perhaps shedding needles upon the floor.

Almost inevitably there is an emotional letdown after
such high expectations and frenetic activity—shopping,
eating, worship services, family reunions, and partings. But

the Church seeks to keep the season going. Again, the Church anticipates this psychology; it understands that there is a need to unwind in the days following the high observance and the pressures of the secular world that spring from the sacred purpose of the holiday.

Hence the 12-day cycle of Christmas from December 25 to January 6.

THE 12 DAYS OF CHRISTMAS

The day *after* Christmas holds its own place in Church and secular observance as well—as if we are not all exhausted after the buildup to Christmas and the climactic celebrations of the day itself.

In the United Kingdom and many of its former colonies throughout the world, December 26 is known as Boxing Day. This is traditionally the day on which the collection or "poor" boxes in the parish church are opened and their contents distributed to the needy. It is a day on which gifts are exchanged among family members and a time to offer gifts—such as tips—to letter carriers, sanitation workers, newspaper delivery folks, doormen, and other service workers. The Boxing Day tradition stems from the much earlier tradition of celebrating the memorial of St. Stephen, the first Christian martyr and one of the first seven deacons (from the Greek *diakonia,* meaning "servant") ordained by the Christian Church (*cf.* Acts 6:1–5). Deacons such as Stephen were responsible for distributing the Church's treasure among its members, especially widows and the poor. So it is in imitation of this central mission of the early Christians that the needy are remembered and served on the day after the Nativity. This theme of charity is also illustrated in a Christmas carol that virtually everyone knows and can hum by heart "Good King Wenceslaus," who performs acts of charity "on the Feast of Stephen."

Subsequent days each hold meaning in the season, calling attention to theological teachings of the Church as well as the lives of significant saints and martyrs.

The first Sunday after Christmas is designated Holy Family Sunday. The Roman Catholic Church considers the nuclear family of Mary, Joseph, and Jesus as the model for all families and sets aside this day to focus on the importance—and the holiness—of the family unit. This is the rough equivalent, for the Church, of Mother's and Father's Days, but, of course, celebrating the whole gang.

December 28 is the Feast of the Holy Innocents. Remember Matthew's Gospel account of the events following Jesus' birth (Matthew 2:13–18)? After the Magi departed Judea without reporting to Herod, who was seeking information on the birth of a potential rival, the king responded like the tyrant he was:

When they [the three wise men] had departed, behold, the angel of the Lord appeared to Joseph in a dream and said, "Rise, take

the child and his mother, flee to Egypt, and stay there until I tell
you. Herod is going to search for the child to destroy him." Joseph
rose and took the child and his mother by night and departed for
Egypt. . . .

When Herod realized that he had been deceived by the magi,
he became furious. He ordered the massacre of all the boys in
Bethlehem and its vicinity two years old and under, in accordance
with the time he had ascertained from the magi.

Then was fulfilled what had been said through Jeremiah
the prophet: "A voice was heard in Ramah, sobbing and loud
lamentation; Rachel weeping for her children, and she would not
be consoled, since they were no more."

Then, when Herod died, the angel directed Joseph to
bring his wife, Mary, and child, Jesus, back to Israel. They
settled in a town called Nazareth in the region of the Galilee.

This feast day is a solemn one, recalling the slaughter of
uncounted children at the whim of a mad ruler who could
have snuffed out the life of the Anointed One, but for the
intervention of an angel and the willingness of the Savior's
"adoptive" father to act at a moment's notice.

December 31 is another important vigil, celebrated
around the world as New Year's Eve. In secular terms, this
holiday is one of the biggest and brightest, bringing out couples and individuals to formal and informal parties in virtually every corner of the country, including huge crowds in
New York City's Times Square. Broadcasters and entertain-

ers come out of the woodwork for the occasion, giving it high media visibility. However, an increasing number of communities across the United States in recent years have tried to reclaim the holiday by holding family-friendly and booze-free "First Night" festivities, emphasizing arts, children's activities, and grass-roots entertainment. The Church also encourages observance of the secular New Year with prayer and reflection, and emphasizes the family component of the holiday as a natural, temporal extension of Christmas.

January 1 is designated as the Feast of Mary the Mother of God (since Vatican II) and the day of Christ's circumcision. The Catechism of the Catholic Church states: "Mary is truly 'Mother of God' since she is the mother of the eternal Son of God made man, who is God himself." The first day of the year is the first of many feasts dedicated to the Blessed Virgin. It is also the first day of the new year on the Gregorian calendar. The liturgical color of the priest's vestments and church decorations is white during this holiday, in keeping with the entire Christmas season.

What about the circumcision? According to Jewish law, the male child is to be circumcised eight days after birth. "This is a liturgical sign of the Old covenant God has made with his chosen People through Abraham (*cf.* Genesis 17:10–14). According to Meridith Gould, author of *The Catholic Home,* after Christ has died and risen, St. Paul will challenge the practice (*cf.* Romans 2:25–28 and Philippians 3) and

Baptism will take its place as evidence of the New Covenant in Christ." The circumcision is also tied to the naming of the child, but since Jesus received his name before his birth, that aspect of the liturgical practice is not generally emphasized.

A significant saint's day in this octave is January 4, the memorial of St. Elizabeth Ann Bayley Seton, the first native-born American saint. She is credited with founding the first Catholic schools in the United States in the early nineteenth century, which eventually became the largest private schooling system in the world, educating millions of young Americans—Catholic and non-Catholic alike. Seton had married into the prominent Bayley family of New York (also related to the Roosevelts), but she came to know poverty and despair as a young widow and mother thrown back on her own resources. She converted to Catholicism and offered herself to John Carroll of Baltimore, the first bishop in the United States. She is also the foundress of the Sisters of Charity, based in suburban Convent Station, New Jersey, at the site of the College of Saint Elizabeth.

Mother Seton's nephew, James Roosevelt Bayley, also converted from Episcopalianism to Catholicism and became the first bishop of Newark, New Jersey. He named the college he founded there after her: Seton Hall University. She was canonized by Pope Paul VI in 1975.

The final day of the Christmas cycle of 12 days is known as the Feast of the Epiphany, the Adoration of the Magi, and sometimes the Feast of the Three Kings. It is celebrated on

January 6, or, more commonly these days, on the closest Sunday.

Epiphany means "appearance" or "manifestation," signifying a revelation of something new. In the Roman tradition this observance revolves around the visit of the Magi to the child Jesus. In the Orthodox tradition the holy day is celebrated primarily because of the baptism of Jesus, where the Holy Spirit appeared, and because of his first miracle at the wedding feast at Cana, where he famously turned water into wine at the suggestion of his mother. On both those occasions, the Lord's divinity was revealed in epiphanies that are both miraculous and very human and earthbound.

In the Catholic tradition, the Feast of the Epiphany is followed, one week later, by a Sunday devoted to the Baptism of the Lord. That other revelation of Christ's divinity, therefore—when he was baptized in the Jordan River as an adult, before he began his public ministry, by his cousin, John the Baptist—takes a suitably prominent place on the Church's calendar during this season.

By the time the Christmas season officially ends and Christmas trees and lights have long since been taken down, secular society has long since moved on. But each autumn, well before Thanksgiving—even right up against Halloween—the drums start beating to announce new products (especially toys), discounts and sales, and those decreasing number of "shopping days 'til Xmas."

The circle remains unbroken.

THE PRESENTATION OF THE LORD,
OR CANDLEMAS, FEBRUARY 2

Forty days after the birth of a Jewish child, parents in Israel of old brought the infant to the temple in Jerusalem to be presented to the elders there. Under the law, from the time of Moses (Leviticus 12:2–8), a woman was considered "unclean" in these 40 days, unable to participate in any religious ritual or touch anyone else who might, and she too was required to present herself to the priests in the temple for purification. Interestingly, this was the practice for a male child—the unclean period was doubled after the birth of a female child!

The Gospel of Luke (2:22–39) contains the full narrative of the event, which is fascinating:

> *When the days were completed for their purification according to the law of Moses, they took him up to Jerusalem to present him to the Lord, just as it is written in the law of the Lord, "Every male that opens the womb shall be consecrated to the Lord," and to offer the sacrifice of a "pair of turtledoves or two young pigeons," in accordance with the dictate in the law of the Lord.*
>
> *Now there was a man in Jerusalem whose name was Simeon. This man was righteous and devout, awaiting the consolation of Israel, and the Holy Spirit was upon him. It had been revealed to him by the Holy Spirit that he should not see death before he had seen the Messiah of the Lord.*

He came in the spirit into the temple, and when the parents brought in the child Jesus to perform the custom of the law in regard to him, he took him into his arms and blessed God, saying "Now, Master, you may let your servant go in peace, according to your word, for my eyes have seen your salvation, for which you prepared in sight of all the peoples, a light for revelation to the Gentiles, and glory for your people Israel."

The child's father and mother were amazed at what was said about him, and Simeon blessed them and said to Mary, his mother: "Behold this child is destined for the fall and rise of many in Israel, and to be a sign that will be contradicted (and you yourself a sword will pierce) so that the thoughts of many hearts may be revealed."

There was also a prophetess, Anna, the daughter of Phanuel, of the tribe of Asher. She was advanced in years, having lived seven years with her husband after her marriage and then as a widow until she was 84. She never left the temple, but worshiped night and day with fasting and prayer. And coming forward at that very time, she gave thanks to God and spoke about the child to all who were awaiting the redemption of Israel.

When they had fulfilled all the prescriptions of the law of the Lord, they returned to Galilee, to their own town of Nazareth.

As the date of the celebration of Christ's birthday had settled at December 25 in the Western churches, February 2 became the date on which the Presentation is observed.

Why is it called Candelmas? Pope Sergius (687–701), late in his reign, instituted a candlelight procession on the day to highlight Simeon's prophecy, which eventually became an occasion for the blessing and distribution of beeswax candles to church members and for use in the sanctuary of the church building. The prayers of the day—and during processions and ceremonies—are antiphons (short sung Scripture verses) and canticles (longer liturgical songs, also sourced from Scripture) dedicated to Mary and to light.

Michael Foley, in his book *Why Do Catholics Eat Fish on Friday?: The Catholic Origin to Just About Everything,* offers an excellent, concise explanation of the tie between Candelmas and the popular phenomenon assigned to the same day, known as Groundhog Day:

> Simeon's prophecy and the focus on light eventually led to a folk belief that the weather on February 2 had a particularly keen prognostic value. If the sun shone for the greater part of the day, there would be, it was claimed, 40 more days of winter, but if the skies were cloudy and gray, there would be an early spring.
>
> The Germans amended this lore by bringing into the equation either the badger or the hedgehog (not to mention their shadows); yet when they emigrated to Pennsylvania in colonial times, they could find no such creatures around. Instead they saw plenty of what the Na-

tive Americans in the area called a wojak, or woodchuck [or groundhog].

And thus "Punxsutawney Phil," as the furry fellow is known, is called upon each year to determine the length of the balance of the winter season. Although he has no divine attributes and is not known to be a Catholic, Phil embodies the melding of traditional lore and the spiritual yearning for the end of winter and the promise of a new season.

"THE TWELVE DAYS OF CHRISTMAS"

A spiritual reading of the famous, merry Christmas song offers some different insights.

> On the first day of Christmas, my true love gave to me a partridge in a pear tree.
> On the second day of Christmas, my true love gave to me two turtledoves.
> On the third day of Christmas, my true love gave to me three French hens.
> On the fourth day of Christmas, my true love gave to me four calling birds.
> On the fifth day of Christmas, my true love gave to me five golden rings.
> On the sixth day of Christmas, my true love gave to me six geese a-laying.
> On the seventh day of Christmas, my true love gave to me seven swans a-swimming.
> On the eighth day of Christmas, my true love gave to me eight maids a-milking.
> On the ninth day of Christmas, my true love gave to me nine ladies dancing.
> On the tenth day of Christmas, my true love gave to me ten lords a-leaping.
> On the eleventh day of Christmas, my true love gave to me eleven pipers piping.
> On the twelfth day of Christmas, my true love gave to me twelve drummers drumming.

The first seven gifts of the twelve days are all birds, if "five golden rings" are interpreted as golden ring-necked pheasants. "Calling birds" is a corruption of "colly birds," which are blackbirds. "Two turtledoves," of course, refer to the sacrifice at the Presentation in the temple. Seven is a divine number, sacred in ancient Israel, and birds are symbols of the soul, such as the image of the Holy Spirit as a dove. The remaining five are human beings full of energy, dancing and leaping (as well as milking). Five, too, has scriptural significance, as in the five books of Moses in the Bible.

In this understanding, according to Laurence Hull Stookey, author of *Calendar: Christ's Time for the Church*, "my true love" is meant as God, the ultimate giver of gifts and creator of life itself. Of course the total of 12 signifies the 12 Apostles and the 12 months of the year. The 12 gifts of these days represent the variety and bounty of God's generosity—and his "true love" for those he is said to have created in his image and likeness.

CHAPTER 4

ST. VALENTINE'S, ST. PATRICK'S, AND ST. JOSEPH'S DAYS

From January through March, Catholics remember abbots, virgins, bishops, and martyrs—among others—on their calendar of saints. But important "secular saints" are also commemorated in this period on the calendar with holidays attached. January 15 is the birthday of the late Dr. Martin Luther King, Jr., the civil rights leader who was assassinated in 1968. Now the third Monday in January, generally within a few days of King's actual birthday, is observed as a national holiday. Many churches (Catholic and Protestant alike) hold special prayer services on this day.

Presidents Day is celebrated in the United States on the Monday after the third Sunday of February. Long ago (that is, until the last quarter of the twentieth century), President Abraham Lincoln's birthday, February 12, was a national holiday, as was President George Washington's birthday on February 22. The combined holiday covers both and is the occasion for department store and automobile "sales events" that dominate the commercial airwaves. There are fewer patriotic events, but there are still some quiet public observances on this midwinter weekend.

ST. VALENTINE'S DAY, FEBRUARY 14

It's ironic that one of the more popular holidays in America is named for a saint about whom very little is known. In fact, the feast day of St. Valentine is no longer recognized in the current Roman calendar. It was removed after the calendar was revised in 1969 by Pope Paul VI. Many saints lost their place in the calendar because not enough information existed to document their lives and sainthood. St. Valentine was a casualty of that revision and lost his place in the official Catholic canon.

The confusion about St. Valentine begins with reports that there may have been two Valentines who lived and died at the same time—one was a priest in Rome and the other was a bishop in Terne, sixty miles outside of Rome (but again, that information is inconclusive). Some scholars believe that there was only one Valentine—that first he was a priest who then became a bishop. And that theory does make sense, since it was also reported that both Valentines were beheaded.

In pagan Rome, February 15 was the feast of the Lupercalia in honor of the pastoral god Lupercus. The Romans performed a ritual meant to ward off wolves, in which men wore strips of animal hide, dancing and cavorting; in mixed company, it evolved into a fertility ritual. Wolves stayed away and love blossomed! The night before the feast, young people used to declare their love for one another or propose marriage. They also used to pledge their companionship and affection to a prospective spouse for the next 12 months, with a view toward marriage. It is this custom that provides the original meaning of being someone's "Valentine."

And where does love enter Valentine's story? Well, all the stories of saints and martyrs have strong elements that describe their great love for God and, in the case of the martyrs, their willingness to sacrifice their lives for this love and commitment. In the story of St. Valentine, he both lived and died for love.

Valentine was a priest in A.D. 269 under the rule of Emperor Claudius II, who is reported to have banned marriage because he believed that single men made better soldiers. But love finds a way, and those who wanted to marry found an ally in the priest Valentine, who agreed to secretly perform the sacrament. When Claudius discovered this treason he imprisoned Valentine. One legend says that young children passed him notes through the prison bars, which could have been the beginning of the custom of sending love notes on Valentine's Day. The priest was eventually beheaded and then named a martyr because he gave up his life to perform the sacrament of marriage: for love of love and love of God.

Medieval authors told stories about St. Valentine as a matchmaker for devout Christian couples. According to one tale, the custom of sharing cards on Valentine's Day echoes a letter that Valentine wrote to his jailer's daughter, whom he had miraculously cured of blindness, shortly before his execution by the Roman authorities. It is said that he signed the note, "'Your Valentine.'"

The great English poet Geoffrey Chaucer, who lived in the fourteenth century and is famous for his *Canterbury Tales,* is credited with calling February 14 "Valentine's Day," the day of love, in his poem "The Parliament of Fowls":

> *For this was on St. Valentine's Day*
> *When every fowl cometh there to*
> *Choose his mate.*

He named the day a symbol of spring and love, with birds billing and cooing.

Shakespeare also refers to Valentine's Day in *A Midsummer Night's Dream* and in *Hamlet:*

> *Good morrow! 'Tis St. Valentine's Day*
> *All in the morning betime,*

And I a maid at yon window,
To be your Valentine!

Here Shakespeare is referring to an English and Italian custom in which single women sat at their windows on Valentine's Day, believing that the first man they saw would be their true love.

Valentine died not knowing that his name would be associated with this happy and intense emotion for centuries to come. Love is worth celebrating—it is probably the best thing to celebrate. The greeting card, flower, and candy industries love, love, love St. Valentine, for he provides substantial cash flow in the first quarter of the year, the first major spending holiday after Christmas.

ST. PATRICK'S DAY, MARCH 17

Everyone is Irish for a day on this holiday honoring the saint who is credited with converting all of Ireland to Christianity.

We do not know exactly when St. Patrick was born, nor exactly where he was born. We do not know when he came to Ireland as a missionary bishop, nor exactly when he died. However, we do know more about him than virtually anyone else of his era because he left behind two documents that are remarkable records of his inner life, as well as his mission among the valiant Irish people. Thus we can safely place him in and around the middle of the fifth century.

Patrick was not himself Irish. He was a Roman citizen born in Britain (possibly in modern-day Wales or Scotland—or even Brittany in northern France) to a well-to-do family. His father was a deacon of the Church and a tax collector. Patrick's grandfather was a Catholic priest, and evidence suggests that his mother was a niece of a revered French saint, Martin of Tours.

None of his wealth and connections protected Patrick from Irish coastal raiders when he was 16 years old; he was kidnapped, taken to Ireland, and held as a slave for six years. Working day and night as a cow or sheep herder, the young man was cut off from home and family and the Christian faith of his childhood, which to that point he had not taken seriously. In the cold and rain, on the rugged hillsides of Ireland, out of desperation and in fear for his life, Patrick experienced a true conversion to the faith of his fathers and began a lifelong commitment to prayer.

After a miraculous escape from slavery and years of studying for the priesthood, Patrick was ordained a priest, and then consecrated a bishop. He had heard voices calling him back to the Ireland of his captivity to bring Christ to the natives, which he proceeded to do—with a vengeance.

In his short autobiography *Confession* and in a letter he wrote to the soldiers of a Christian warlord, St. Patrick expressed in no uncertain terms the depth of his faith and his fierce determination to answer the call he felt came directly from God. This angered some of his brethren, who accused him of overreaching his authority and even accepting money, as well as having inappropriate relationships with women. Patrick successfully defended himself against the charges, leaving historians with the impression that his colleagues' primary motivation in their attacks was jealousy of his success.

Patrick was taking the Gospel to what he thought were "the farthest ends of the earth," believing (as had St. Paul) that he was living at the end of time. Upon his death, he was acclaimed a saint by the locals. This form of sainthood was the custom for hundreds of years of Church history before canonization was formalized and centralized in the Vatican. It is clear that Patrick's vivid personality had a huge impact on everyone around him.

The Irish diaspora during the nineteenth-century potato famine brought hundreds of thousands of immigrants to American shores along with their Catholic faith and a fondness for both ale and their patron saint. Today, parades and celebrations are held in nearly every city in the United States, and the holiday is a boon for manufacturers of green hats and green beer.

"Erin go bragh" and "Top o' the morning" are spoken on his day, and corned beef and cabbage served, which provides some relief from the winter doldrums and is often a welcome interruption in the bleak Lenten landscape for Catholics, whether or not they are of Irish descent.

ST. JOSEPH'S DAY, MARCH 19

Known as the "foster father" of Jesus, Joseph is also the patron of the universal Catholic Church, a title bestowed on him by Pope Pius IX. The Solemnity of St. Joseph, Husband of the Virgin Mary, originated sometime before the tenth century, and since Pope Paul VI's revision of the Church calendar in 1969, has been fixed on March 19. In addition, and in recognition of Joseph's status in the Holy Family, Italy, Spain, and Portugal celebrate March 19 as Father's Day. Also, the month of March is dedicated to him by the Roman Catholic Church.

St. Joseph was a carpenter (*cf.* Matthew 13:55), and as such is the patron saint of carpenters, as well as religious orders. His is one of the most popular names for Catholic parents to name their sons, and statues of Joseph and the child Jesus are ubiquitous in churches and Catholic schools everywhere.

Joseph's popularity has waxed and waned throughout history, but he holds special significance in the Italian, Maltese, and Filippino cultures. In Italy, San Giuseppe is credited with saving Sicily from famine during medieval times by bringing rain to the people who had prayed to him. Many Italian village parishes celebrate St. Joseph's day with festivals that include altar decorations of flowers and candles, and abundant gifts of wines, cakes, and breads, and the wearing of red or purple clothing. Fava beans are associated with St. Joseph as the crop that he saved in his "intervention" in Sicily. Zeppole di San Giuseppe is a popular type of cream puff with ricotta cheese stuffing in Italy, and meatless dishes are popular for this holiday. However, since the holiday is during Lent, if it falls on a Friday, the local diocese may lift the Church rule of abstinence.

In the Philippines, many families keep a tradition in which an old man, a young lady, and a small boy are chosen and dressed up as St. Joseph, the Blessed Virgin Mary, and the child Jesus. They are seated around a table set with the family's best silver and china and served a variety of courses, sometimes being spoon-fed by family members, while a prayer to St. Joseph is recited at a temporary home altar erected for the day.

One of the most remarkable aspects of St. Joseph's Day is that it marks the return of migrant cliff swallows to the Mission of San Juan Capistrano in California. The mission is one of the oldest buildings in California, built in 1776 and founded by the Franciscans, who are known in part for their friendly treatment of all animal creatures. Each year on October 23, the birds, known locally as *las golondrinas,* fly south to Argentina, a journey of some 7500 miles. They always return on or around March 19.

A portion of a novena to St. Joseph, a prayer to be said once a day for nine days, beginning on the vigil of the feast day itself, illustrates the reverence in which this figure is held by many Catholics:

O glorious descendant of the kings of Judah, inheritor of the virtues of all the patriarchs. Just and happy St. Joseph, listen to my prayer. You are my glorious protector, and shall ever be, after Jesus and Mary the object of my most profound veneration and confidence. You are the most hidden, though the greatest saint, and are particularly the patron of those who serve God with the greatest purity and fervor. In union with all those who have ever been most devoted to you I now dedicate myself to your service; beseeching you, for the sake of Jesus Christ, who vouchsafed to love and obey you as a son, to become a father to me, and to obtain for me that filial respect, confidence, and love of a child toward you.

THE LITURGICAL AND
SPIRITUAL YEAR

Time can be seen as a circle, a cycle that unfolds in a continuum linked at the beginning and ending of the solar year's 365 days. In our daily lives there are beginnings and endings, weeks and months, seasons and years, but any individual human being can experience it only one moment at a time, with memory and anticipation bridging past days and the unknowable future.

The Catholic faith promises the believer an experience beyond the empirical, outside the strict boundaries of space and time. It is a spiritual experience of what is called "salvation history." What does this mean, and how does one express such a concept in a way that is understandable to the imperfect and limited human mind? The key is to appeal in such matters to the mind *through* the soul.

Thus, spiritual concepts and meanings are expressed, in the Catholic tradition, through art and literature, through memory and festival, through the marking of time in days

and seasons that give some structure to the chaos that life
can become. Think especially of the so-called dark ages in
Europe and near Asia during the period following the col-
lapse of imperial authority in the West and constant war-
fare throughout the world that the Roman Empire had once
encompassed and controlled.

The calendar developed by Julius Caesar survived him
by many hundreds of years, as did the generally accepted
view of time. Similarly, the Catechism of the Catholic
Church offers guidance regarding the beliefs and practices
revealed through time. "In Jesus 'the kingdom of God is at
hand.' (*cf.* Mark 1:15) He calls his hearers to conversion and
faith, but also to *watchfulness*"—over time. In other words:
The liturgical year is itself a prayer, a response to the Savior's
call and commission to his followers.

The Liturgy of the Hours is the daily prayer cycle in
which ordained clergy, professed religious (i.e., monks and
nuns), and lay Catholics throughout the world participate
together. At any moment of any day there are hundreds
of thousands of voices, raised in a particular prayer to a
common God. Multiply this day by seven or by 365. Each
hour, then, and each day achieve a value in the chronicle
of that kingdom to come. The Catechism of the Catholic
Church states it this way:

The hymns and litanies of the Liturgy of the Hours integrate the
prayer of the psalms into the age of the Church, expressing the

symbolism of the time of day, the liturgical season, or the feast being celebrated.

Moreover, the reading from the Word of God at each Hour (with the subsequent responses or troparia*) and readings from the Fathers and spiritual masters at certain hours, reveal more deeply the meaning of the mystery being celebrated, assist in understanding the psalms, and prepare for silent prayer.*

The lectio divina, *where the Word of God is so read and meditated that it becomes prayer, is thus rooted in the liturgical celebration.*

Thus the liturgical year is also, in its practical application, the cross on which the Body of Christ (a familiar theological trope for the Church) hangs securely.

SUNDAY AND THE WEEK

Taken directly from the account of God's creation of the world found in the Book of Genesis, the idea of dividing time by days—from one sunset to another to another, and so on—has been fixed in cultures around the world. All three major Abrahamic religions—Judaism, Christianity, and Islam—count time in groups of seven days, which we call a week.

As the First Day inaugurates—and sanctifies—the week, so the Lord's Day has priority in and determines the liturgical year. The highest holy day of the year, Easter, is observed on a *Sunday,* unlike Christmas, which is celebrated on a particular date, not tied to any day of the week.

THE SEASON OF ADVENT

In the language of the Mass, "we wait in joyful hope for the coming of our Savior, Jesus Christ." So, in the spirit of anticipation that marks each celebration of the Catholic Mass, a period within the year, beginning four Sundays before Christmas Day, is set aside to focus on this aspect of Christian life. Readings from the prophet Isaiah and other prophets reinforce the notion that the Jews, as the Chosen People, awaited Christ's coming for centuries.

CHRISTMAS SEASON

The full Christmas season lasts from Christmas Eve (December 24) to the third Sunday after Christmas, the celebration of the Feast of the Baptism of the Lord, a period lasting two to three weeks and encompassing the 12 Days of Christmas.

The Messiah, or Savior, subjected himself to the full cycle of human life: birth as well as death. Yet he remained fully divine, according to the teaching of the Church. It is, of course, an old and familiar story: No room at the inn, swaddling clothes, angels, shepherds, and visiting wise men. Still, there is a freshness and hope about the Nativity story and the attendant celebration, especially in the eyes and hearts of children. The universal appeal of Charles Dickens' *A Christmas Carol* is powerful testimony to the power of this great season to melt even the hardest of hearts.

THE SEASON OF LENT

The Church encourages its membership to get serious during this period of 40 days, which represents two biblical episodes: the Jews' 40 years of wandering after their exodus from slavery in Egypt, and Christ's 40 days of wandering, at the behest of the Holy Spirit, in the desert before the inauguration of his active ministry.

Lent is derived from Easter and secondary to it. According to the theologian Laurence Hull Stookey, "Briefly put, Lent is like an ellipse: It is a single entity with a double focus. The forty days are (a) a time for a probing consideration of our human condition, including sin and its deadly consequences for other individuals and society, and (b) a time for an equally intense consideration of the new possibilities offered to us in Jesus Christ and their implications for practical living."

Lent is, then, primarily a 40-day journey of the soul through fasting and prayer, as if the entire Church is united in solemn focus on what is to come: the fulfillment of the promises of the prophets and the yearnings of the people. It is a quiet time at the ending of the dark season of winter and the dawn of the new season—and renewed life—of spring.

THE PASCHAL TRIDUUM

Concentrated in three days (hence the Latin "triduum"), this brief period covers Holy Thursday, Good Friday, and Holy Saturday. It runs from the day of Jesus' Passover supper ("pasch" is the Greek rendering of "Passover") with his Apostles, to his passion (trials and suffering), to his crucifixion, death, and burial in the tomb. These holy days are the darkest and most solemn in the Church's calendar.

At the Easter Vigil Mass, new members of the Church are initiated in the sacrament of Baptism and Confirmation and celebrate the sacrament of the Eucharist (Holy Communion) for the first time. This is yet another ancient custom, that of the *neophytes*, the newcomers to the Christian fold who were highlighted and welcomed visibly in the churches of the early centuries of Christianity.

This shortest "mini-season," if you will, is packed with liturgical significance for the entire year, and yet it's concentrated within 48 hours over a span of three days.

EASTER SEASON

Following the most solemn season comes the most joyous of them all. Easter rings with "alleluias," proclamations of joy, for 50 days. From Easter Sunday through the Solemnity of Pentecost, the fasts of Lent are replaced with feasts and celebrations. The priest blesses the people with water at every Sunday Mass during this period.

Christians hold fast to the belief that "Christ is risen." Here, in the Scripture readings on Sundays and every day through the week, the story of the resurrection and the foundation of the Catholic Church by Christ's followers are recounted. Again, the basis for this season can be traced to the Jewish festival of 50 days that began two days after Passover and lasted until the Day of Pentecost. Just like the number 7, the number 50 carries theological meaning: the period of a "jubilee," as reflected in Leviticus, Easter represents a distinct continuity between Jewish and Christian traditions, and points to the deep common roots of the two monotheistic faiths that ought not to be minimized in Catholics' thinking and practices.

ORDINARY TIME

The longest "season," which is really no season at all, but known simply as Ordinary Time, stretches from the commemoration of the "birthday of the Church" on Pentecost in late May or early June all the way to the Saturday following Christ the King Sunday in November.

Nonetheless, Ordinary Time is chock-full of solemnities, feasts, and memorials of the Lord, the Virgin Mary, and the many saints. Saints' days are not dependent upon any particular season but are spread over the entire year in what is called the "sanctoral cycle," and may be preempted by the holy day observances not tied to particular dates (an example of this would be Good Friday).

The Advent–Christmas and Lent–Easter cycles make up almost exactly half of the solar year, balanced by Ordinary Time, which represents the second half. The use of the term "ordinary" derives from the use of ordinal (i.e., "counting") numbers to mark the Sundays during this lengthy stretch of time—roughly from June through November, along with that shorter span between Christmas and Lent.

What does this all add up to for the observant Catholic, the faithful Christian, or the secularly oriented person? Well, we are now living in an age dominated by instant electronic communication that has significantly—and perhaps permanently—affected our experience of time. Of all the forces in the world that have separated persons from traditional religious belief and practice, technology is one of the most powerful. Now we are well accustomed to the 24/7 cycle of news, information, stock trading, work, play, travel, and shopping. Through the Internet we can access practically anything or conduct any kind of business at any time of night or day.

This technological revolution has "conquered," or perhaps "mastered" time in new ways and widens the gap between the purely practical and secular understanding of time and the more traditional, sacred meanings. Persons of faith must therefore cling a bit more tenaciously to traditions that have become "outdated" in our contemporary society.

Today, priests carry the same message in the pulpit that they have for decades: Keep holy the day of the Lord. Many Catholics do. Statistically, many more Catholics do not. The pace of life has accelerated to the point of frenzy for so many in all strata of society. That is simply the way it is.

The Church, however, remains anchored in history, even as it seeks to exist, untethered, between heaven and earth. The liturgical year, therefore, imposes a structure on the experience of earthly time as it unfurls throughout the natural year of four seasons, heat and cold, planting and harvest, life and death.

DEDICATIONS THROUGHOUT THE YEAR

Month	Dedicated to
January	Holy Name and Childhood of Jesus
February	The Holy Family
March	St. Joseph
April	Blessed Sacrament
May	Blessed Virgin Mary
June	Sacred Heart of Jesus
July	Most Precious Blood of Christ
August	Immaculate Heart of Mary
September	The Seven Sorrows (Dolours) of Mary
October	The Holy Rosary (and the Holy Angels)
November	Poor Souls in Purgatory
December	Immaculate Conception

THE LECTIONARY

The lectionary is the cycle of Scripture readings from year to year and within a given year. It is the goal of the Catholic Church to present the Bible in its entirety to the faithful in readings at daily and Sunday Mass.

In *Calendar: Christ's Time for the Church,* Laurence Hull Stookey presents a cogent explanation of the modern lectionary:

> Anyone who was active before 1970 [that is, before the litur-
> gical changes mandated by the Second Vatican Council were
> implemented] in churches that observe a calendar can recog-
> nize vast changes that have occurred since then. The extent of
> the changes varies from one denomination to another; but
> the fact of alteration is universal. Nor is it an accident that
> for the 1970 liturgical year, a new lectionary was put in place
> by Roman Catholics. This system of Scripture readings for
> public worship was then altered in relatively slight ways and
> adopted in varying forms by many Protestants.
>
> The question thus arises: Did readings chosen for the new
> lectionary create a different understanding of the meaning of
> observances such as Lent; or did altered understandings of the
> meaning of liturgical time such as Lent dictate which read-
> ings would be chosen for the revised lectionary. The only sat-
> isfactory answer is "Both."

This practice of a universal book of daily and seasonal readings dates back to ancient times, specifically designed for Lenten instruction of catechumens as they approached the baptismal font and full membership in the Church.

PART II

SPRING

In spring, the cycle of life kicks into gear. It is the season of renewal and birth—of light, water, flowers, the emergence of animal life from winter's cold and darkness. The spring equinox breaks the grip of winter on the Northern Hemisphere.

For thousands of years, pagan earth religions lifted up their deities in this season, worshiping their power and fecundity, rejoicing in the visible evidence of new life and the fragrances that emerge at this time of the year. It is a time of sowing and a time of hope.

Based on the Jewish observance of Passover (in late March or early April in the Julian and Gregorian calendars of the West), the Christian tradition of Easter became, over two millennia, the fulcrum of the faith. Our increasingly secular culture has, in recent decades—arguably over the past few *centuries* since the Enlightenment changed the orientation of intellectual development in the West—pushed many religious meanings and assumptions aside.

Easter, the high point of spring for believers, has endured as a breaking of time: a period for school vacations and family reunions. Easter egg hunts and the Easter Rabbit have, indeed, superseded the religious holy day for many. And for others, Major League Baseball's opening day is the highest holy day of all!

CHAPTER 5

LENT

A mirror of Advent, Lent is an especially intense period of 40 days in anticipation of Easter. It is a time of prayer, abstinence, penance, and a focus on doing good works as necessary forms of spiritual preparation for the highest of high holy days in the Christian calendar.

Lent is a breaking of time, a breaking of one's routine. Originally, "Lent," from the German, meant simply the spring season. In Latin, the term *quadragesima* was applied to this time period, meaning, also quite simply, the "forty days" or the "fortieth day." In the Romance languages that stemmed from Latin, it is easy to see the derivative words: in French, *carême;* in Italian, *quaresima;* and in Spanish, *cuaresma.* In Greek, the term is *tessarakoste* (fortieth), which is analogous to *pentekoste* (or Pentecost, for fiftieth).

Some Church Fathers as early as the fifth century believed that the fast of 40 days had been instituted in the time of the Apostles. Scholars today dispute that position, pointing to the diverse practices regarding the fast before Easter during the preceding centuries. The earliest known mention of Lent occurs in Eusebius' history of the Church, *Historia Ecclesiastica*. He quotes from a letter to Pope St. Victor I from St. Irenaeus, the second-century bishop of Lyons, a disciple of Polycarp (a follower of the Apostle John the Evangelist).

Irenaeus acknowledges a long-standing controversy of the time, keeping Easter, as well as the duration of the period of fasting before Easter. "The dispute is not only about the day, but about the actual character of the fast. Some think that they ought to fast for one day, some for two, others for still more. Some make their 'day' last 40 hours on end. Such variation in the observance did not originate in our own day, but very much earlier, in the time of our forefathers."

Two centuries later, when Rufinus translated Eusebius' Greek into Latin, he punctuated the passage so that the critical words would read, "40 days, 24 hours a day."

Tertullian, another of the pre-Nicene Fathers (i.e., those theologians who wrote before the Council of Nicaea in 325) and an important source for so many of the Catholic holy day observances found in this book, wrote of "the days on which the bride groom was taken away" (presumably meaning Good Friday and Holy Saturday, when Jesus lay in the tomb) as a common term of fasting for Christians. But there is little else we can point to that proves there was a full-fledged Lenten fast in his time that had originated during the days of the early Church.

Of course, that did not prevent Pope St. Leo I from preaching that Church members should "fulfill with their fasts the apostolic institution of the 40 days." So in Leo's day, the middle of the fifth century (supported during that time by another authoritative writer, St. Cyril of Alexandria, in his *Festal Letters*), the practice of a 40-day fast for Lent was firmly established in the Roman Catholic liturgical tradition.

In the fifth canon (i.e., law) that came out of the Council of Nicaea is the first mention of the *tessarakoste*, the 40-day period, before Easter, then after Easter and up to the Feast of the Ascension. During this time Church meetings called synods should not be held. Clearly, the legalisms surrounding the establishment of Lent can give one a headache.

Suffice it to say that by late antiquity, Lent had been confirmed by the teaching of the bishops and the practice of the people in localities throughout the Christian world.

Nowadays, the most common (but by no means universal) practice of the Church, confirmed by each bishop in his own jurisdiction, is to observe the rule of abstinence, including eating no meat on Fridays during Lent and the rule of fasting, which means eating only one meal on both Ash Wednesday and Good Friday. This is the simplest formulation of the regulations, but there are loopholes (for those looking for them): On Sundays and solemnities such as the Feast of St. Joseph (March 19) and the Feast of the Annunciation (March 25), one is technically exempt and can partake of whatever has been offered up for Lent! This is because the Roman Catholic Church skips Sundays when calculating the duration of Lent. (The Orthodox tradition, however, includes the Sundays.)

MARDI GRAS

This is a post-Christmas, pre-Easter carnival observed outside the strictures of the Church and falls on the day *before* Ash Wednesday. The parades and parties of Mardi Gras, or "Fat Tuesday," signal the end of worldly indulgence before the six weeks of solemnity and rigorous abstinence that is Lent.

We think primarily of the lavish, over-the-top celebrations held annually in Rio de Janeiro and New Orleans as representative of this phenomenon today. Both cities become epicenters of publicly sanctioned debauchery and festivity, with local citizens and tourists from around the world joining in. Venice, Italy, too, is well known for its colorful and indulgent carnival season.

During Super Bowl III, New York Jets quarterback Joe Namath stunned the sports world with his promised upset victory, held in New Orleans during carnival. The root of carnival, of course, comes from "flesh" or "meat." And plenty of such consumption was going on down there in the Big Easy before, during, and after that particular Super Bowl.

But carnival actually referred to a more religious time of feasting and merrymaking. Before the season of Lent (and prior to the age of refrigeration), Christians would slowly begin to abstain from cheese, dairy, and meat products—which they would give up completely during the "Great Fast."

Quinquagesima Sunday ("fifty days"—signifying the roughly seven weeks until Easter) was thus called *Domenica Carnevala. Carnevala* was derived from the Latin for "removal" (*levare*) of "meat" (*carno/carnis*), though that meaning would evolve to the sense of bidding good-bye (*vale*) to meat. This voluntary period of pre-fasting would come to be known as pre-Lent and began in the Roman calendar three Sundays before Ash Wednesday, culminating on the Sunday before Lent, Quinquagesima Sunday.

The day is observed in the Church unofficially as Shrove Tuesday. The name comes from the custom of going to confession (i.e., "shrift") before the onset of Lent, in order to unburden the soul of sin before embarking on the path of spiritual cleansing and renewal—carrying less baggage into the "desert" of Lent.

There are a number of food-related customs that go along with Shrove Tuesday. It is also known as "Pancake Tuesday," after the common practice of starting the day with flapjacks. Meredith Gould, in her excellent book of holiday traditions and recipes, *The Catholic Home*, explains:

"In England, Pancake Day is celebrated with races at which women over the age of 16, frying pans in hand, trot over 415 yards while tossing pancakes over at least three times."

The so-called King's Cake is baked in New Orleans for Mardi Gras: A miniature doll of the baby Jesus is baked into the super-sweet cake—whoever comes up with the baby in his or her slice will provide the cake the following year. Similarly, "hodgepodge" is a dish of the day for eastern Europeans, which includes vegetables, potatoes, and pig parts. Traditional soups, too, are popular in Europe and Russia on this day.

Meredith Gould provides the following tidbit, which I find irresistible:

> The pretzel is the oldest, traditional, authentically Christian Lenten bread. Some food historians trace its origin back to Roman Christians of the 5th century. Others insist that monks in southern France, or maybe it was northern Italy, cooked this egg- and butter-free snack up in 610 A.D. The former called them bracellae, Latin for "little arms"; the latter called them pretiola, Latin for "little reward."
>
> In either account, the dough configuration represents arms folded in prayer and the three holes represent the Trinity. Thus, you may eat these with impunity, but not gluttony, throughout Lent . . .
>
> So where does "pretzel" come from? Germans, who called the breads bretzel ("little bread"). And here's information you'll need for future quiz shows: Palatine Germans, who would be-

come known as the Pennsylvania Dutch, imported pretzels to the United States in 1710.

ASH WEDNESDAY

The focus of *Dies Cinerum*—this "Day of Ashes," set on the first day, always a Wednesday, of Lent—is sin, a consistent theme in the Catholic tradition. More specifically, it recalls the original sin of Adam and Eve in the Garden of Eden and God's admonition to them: having created them from the dust of the earth (also his creation), they would surely return to that state of dust and decay because they had disobeyed his single commandment—to not eat from the Tree of Knowledge. That is, before their eventual resurrection and reunion with him and all their progeny at the end of time.

Theologically speaking, the original transgression of the First Couple has marked each of us (with the key exceptions of Jesus of Nazareth and his mother, Mary) and made necessary this whole plan of salvation for which the Church exists in the first place.

That's a lot to think about, and perhaps that is why it is concentrated in a single day with a single familiar ritual that ties all Christians (primarily of the Catholic variety) together: the reception of ashes on the forehead, usually in the form of a cross. With the imposition of the ashes, the minister reminds the penitent of the woeful words of God in Genesis (3:19): "For you are dust, and to dust you shall return."

In the words of Laurence Hull Stookey in *Calendar: Christ's Time for the Church:*

> *Ash Wednesday is intended to be a bold confrontation with death. This is to many in our world a painful dose of reality; for we live in a culture that prefers to ignore death to the fullest extent possible and to dress up that which cannot be concealed. The dying are often sequestered in medical care facilities; and their corpses are displayed in finery and exquisite coffins, but only after the morticians and cosmeticians have made the dead bodies look youthful and vibrant.*
>
> *Then comes the Church and declares brashly once a year: "Face it. You will die and your body will decay. You are powerless to prevent it, and denial will get you nowhere. Even the finest medical technology can do nothing to change the fact that death is exactly what it has always been—one per person. So stop kidding yourself!"*

Ash Wednesday originated in the sixth century A.D. The name *Dies Cinerum* has been found in the earliest copies of the Gregorian Sacramentary (there's that ubiquitous Gregory the Great again). The ashes used in the rite are made from the burnt remains of the palm fronds blessed on the previous year's Palm Sunday.

The custom of distributing ashes on the foreheads of the faithful (and, in olden days, upon the tonsure—or shaved bald spot—of ordained clergy) derived from the early sixth-century practice of public penance. Catholics take the practice to heart. Perhaps some remember the story recorded by the tenth-century author Elfric in his *Lives of the Saints*. He wrote to remind all Christians about how, in both the Old and New Testaments, "the men who repented of their sins bestrewed themselves with ashes and clothed their bodies with sackcloth. Now let us do this little at the beginning of our Lent that we strew ashes upon our heads to signify that we ought to repent of our sins during the Lenten fast."

Elfric goes on to recount the cautionary example of the man who refused to attend church to receive his ashes on Ash Wednesday; a few days later, he was accidentally killed in a boar hunt. So there! (Today the practice is encouraged but not obligatory.)

GETTING SERIOUS ABOUT LENT

All Catholics are encouraged to undertake their own spiritual journey in the season through the exercises of self-denial and spiritual preparation, especially in prayer.

Those who are not yet baptized in the Catholic faith, the so-called catechumens who have been studying the teachings of the Church in the Rite of Christian Initiation for Adults (those over 18 years of age), begin their season of Lent at the Rite of Election, signaling their final preparation for baptism on the Vigil of Easter (the Holy Saturday evening Mass).

The practical result of Lenten observance is thought to be a deepening awareness of one's physical needs and cravings (for candy, alcohol, or favorite foods) through abstinence from them. These, the Church teaches, are impediments or blocks to full acceptance of Christ and a distancing of oneself from God. Lent is all about "dying" to such false gods and "rising" with Christ on Easter.

COLORS

Vestments during Lent on Sundays and for weekdays are violet, a deeper, truer purple than the purple of Advent, which is tinged more strongly with blue (called Sarum blue), to express a deeper sorrow. The fourth Sunday of Lent, at the halfway point, expresses the hope embodied in the season with rose-colored vestments (similar to the third Sunday of Advent). And the final Sunday is Passion or Palm Sunday, calling for the blood-red vesture associated with martyrdom. On three feasts during Lent the priest wears white: the Annunciation of the Lord and the Solemnity of St. Joseph, the stepfather of Jesus.

PRAYERS AND MUSIC

The "official" prayers of the Mass during Lent focus on the penitential rite, that is, the *Kyrie eleison* (Lord, have mercy) and/or the *Confiteor* (I, confess). The *Gloria* (Glory to God) is omitted on the Sundays of Lent and the *Alleluia* is not sung during Lent as the acclamation before the Gospel reading (which is otherwise used throughout the year).

Some churches curtail the use of music during the season, eliminating the recessional or dismissal hymn. Otherwise, the music of Lent includes mournful, hopeful, and penitential psalms and antiphons. The hymns often refer to the 40 days, repentance, and sorrow; some familiar ones are "All Glory, Laud and Honor," "*Stabat Mater,*" and "O Sacred Head Surrounded."

Most Catholic parishes pray the Stations of the Cross at least weekly during Lent. The Stations are the fourteen moments during the Passion of Christ that are represented by pictures or sculptures arrayed around the nave of the church, at which the faithful stop, pray, and reflect, keeping in mind the suffering and death their Savior endured for them—one of the chief themes of the season.

As elsewhere in the Church calendar, this particular season has its frequent and special commemorations of saints throughout the 40 days. In addition to Lenten saints we've already covered (Valentine, Patrick, and Joseph, husband of the Virgin Mary), others stand out for Catholics and non-Catholics alike, each with their own unique stories, including St. Scholastica.

ST. SCHOLASTICA

Practically all the information about St. Scholastica comes from the *Dialogues* of St. Gregory the Great (himself a former monk of the Benedictine rule).

Scholastica was born around A.D. 480 and died on February 10, 547—celebrated as her memorial—and was the sister of St. Benedict of Nursia. She joined him in dedicating her life to prayer and work and is the patron of Benedictine nuns. In fact, according to one hagiographer, "she had been dedicated from her infancy to Our Lord, and used to come once a year to visit her brother. To whom the man of God went not far from the gate to a place that did belong to the abbey, there to give her entertainment."

In a famous story, Benedict refused to extend his customary visit with Scholastica one evening, despite her entreaty. So she prayed and, at the end of a day "when the sky was so clear that no cloud was to be seen," God sent a severe tempest that required her brother to remain. "Neither venerable Benedict, nor the monks that were with him, could put their head out of the door." Benedict stayed, and they enjoyed spiritual conversation, a pastime too rarely pursued in our own high-speed world.

Three days later, Benedict beheld a vision: Scholastica's soul departed from her body in the likeness of a dove, to ascend into heaven. With "hymns and lauds he gave thanks to Almighty God, and did impart the news of her death to his monks whom he sent presently to bring her corpse to his abbey, to have it buried in that grave which he had provided for himself."

Scholastica is the patron of nuns, epileptics, and autistic children, and her intercession is invoked against storms and rain, which she had called down from God in order to keep her reluctant brother and fellow saint in her company for one last conversation together.

CHAPTER 6

HOLY WEEK AND THE TRIDUUM

The Catholic Church has always sought to define, circumscribe, and even govern time in its own way. Holy days and saints' days are the means by which this is accomplished—and larger groupings such as the 12 days of Christmas, the 40 days of Lent, or the 50 days between Easter and Pentecost are other major examples.

There are a number of *octaves,* too, during the liturgical year—meaning an eight-day cycle. More than a week, but much less than a month. Why, then, *eight* days? One of the primary illustrations of this concept is the week-plus of Passion Sunday (familiarly known as Palm Sunday) through Easter Sunday. Except for the Sunday of Easter, the Big One, this observance covers the seven days known as Holy Week.

Fasten your seat belts; this is going to be a bumpy ride. Spiritually and historically, the Church seeks to immerse the faithful in religiosity during the week that builds inexorably toward the most sacred celebration on the calendar.

The secular world takes little notice of this time period (unlike on Ash Wednesday, when participants place a visible black mark upon the forehead). But it frequently coincides with the Jewish celebration of Passover, from which it derives, so Jews may take leave from work for an extra day during this week, even as Catholics may choose to take off Good Friday. Both may be noticeable absences in certain workplaces.

PALM SUNDAY

The sixth and last Sunday of Lent, inaugurating Holy Week, is commemorated as Passion Sunday or Palm Sunday. It is one of the greatest days in the Church calendar—a memorial of the resurrection of Christ and his special place as the son of God, seated at the right hand of the Father as a royal prince.

What is likely the earliest mention of the blessing of the palms and the procession on this day is found in France, in a ninth- or tenth-century Sacramentary. It is also known as "Flower Sunday" in England, Germany (as *Blumentag*), Serbia, Croatia, Ruthenia (modern-day western Ukraine), France (*Pâques fleuries*), and Spain (*Pascua florida*). Other names for this day in England included Blossom, Branch, Olive, Sallow, or Yew Sunday, or the Sunday of the Willow Boughs.

It is worth reading and remembering the narrative from Luke's Gospel (19:28–40) and envisioning the church filled with parishioners holding palm fronds or branches, to be blessed by the priest, which they will carry home with them on this day.

After he had said this, he proceeded on his journey up to Jerusalem. As he drew near to Bethpage and Bethany at the place called the Mount of Olives, he sent two of his disciples.

He said, "Go into the village opposite you, and as you enter it you will find a colt tethered on which no one has ever sat. Untie it and bring it here. And if anyone should ask you, 'Why are you untying it?' you will answer, 'The Master has need of it.'"

So those who had been sent went off and found everything just as he had told them. And as they were untying the colt, its owners said to them, "Why are you untying this colt?" They answered, "The Master has need of it." So they brought it to Jesus, threw their cloaks over the colt, and helped Jesus to mount.

As he rode along, the people were spreading their cloaks on the road; and now as he was approaching the slope of the Mount of Olives, the whole multitude of his disciples began to praise God aloud with joy for all the mighty deeds they had seen. They proclaimed: "Blessed is the king who comes in the name of the Lord. Peace in heaven and glory in the highest."

Some of the Pharisees in the crowd said to him, "Teacher, rebuke your disciples." He said in reply, "I tell you, if they keep silent, the stones will cry out!"

At this point in his journey, approaching Jerusalem, Jesus wept over the city, knowing what was to come. According to the Gospel writer, he foresaw not only his own impending death but also the destruction of the city and the destruction of the temple. All this amid the adulation of the crowd, giving Christ a royal welcome to Israel's holiest city. Remember the Star of Bethlehem and the Magis' mission, and King Herod's fear of a usurper who would claim kingship over the Jews?

The palm branches blessed on this Sunday are seen as emblems of joy and victory (the royal procession of Christ and his victory over death). They are taken home on Palm Sunday and used for the balance of the year as a sacramental, or visible, sign of faith. Traditionally they were preserved prominently in the home or the barn. They were thrown into the fireplace by families during storms to ward off death, and it was a custom of some Germans to decorate the grave with blessed palms. The palms, after all, ensured God's protection of those who lived in a home containing one of these branches.

The same blessed palms are burned to procure the ashes used on Ash Wednesday (thus completing the circle of time from the end of one Lent to the beginning of another).

THE TRIDUUM—THREE DAYS

The Triduum supersedes and replaces every other celebration on the liturgical calendar, including saints' days and even the Solemnity of the Annunciation of the Lord (March 25), if the latter happens to fall within this span of three days.

Laurence Hull Stookey writes that in the early decades of the Church all was done in a single extended service; the separation into parts did not evolve into its present form for centuries. And until recently, the division into parts destroyed the ancient sense of unity; the strange title for these services is an attempt to refocus our attention on that unity. *Triduum* (pronounced TRID-oo-um) is a Latin term meaning "three days." It is a thoroughly "churchy" word, not to be found even in most unabridged dictionaries until very recently. What is important, however, is not that the word be introduced to churchgoers but that the reality of a unified observance spread across three days be evident to those who attend the rites of the Triduum.

The Catechism of the Catholic Church provides its own take on this three-day cycle: "Beginning with the Easter Triduum as its source of light, the new age of Resurrection fills the whole liturgical year with its brilliance. Gradually, on either side of this source, the year is transfigured by the liturgy. . . . The economy of salvation is at work within the framework of time, but since its fulfillment in the Passover of Jesus and the outpouring of the Holy Spirit, the culmination of history is anticipated 'as a foretaste,' and the kingdom of God enters into our time."

Again, the concept of the "breaking of time" is brought forward in the Triduum, wedged as it is between the final holy days of Lent and the explosion of grace on the "Great Sunday," Easter. The previous rule of time is frankly set aside.

HOLY THURSDAY

On Holy Thursday, the only Mass held is in the evening (unlike most weekdays and Saturdays in most parishes and dioceses, on which morning and evening Masses are commonly celebrated), to commemorate the "Lord's Supper," or the Last Supper as it is most often called. (Leonardo da Vinci's famous—or now perhaps infamous—painting leaps immediately to mind in this regard.)

The name "Maundy Thursday" comes from the Latin *Mandatum*, or "mandate"—the first words of the Office of the Washing of the Feet in which Jesus admonishes his followers to do this as he has done it in service to others.

The ceremony of the washing of the feet is, strictly speaking, optional, but is included in most Holy Thursday liturgies. The holy oils used in the sacraments of the Church (blessed at the Chrism Mass celebrated at the cathedral) are presented with the gifts of bread and wine during the offertory of the Mass on Holy Thursday.

The Gloria is brought back for a one-night-only appearance on this night.

GOOD FRIDAY

From the earliest days of the Church, Christians kept every Friday as a feast day, in preparation for the Sabbath, so the Friday marking Jesus' death is a unique and special day. Mass is not celebrated on the Friday of Holy Week, which is called "Good Friday" to emphasize the result of the suffering and death of Christ. Instead, Catholics meet without Mass but with Scripture readings, lessons, lengthy prayers, and ceremonials.

There is no more solemn day of the year than this.

The adoration of the cross, symbolizing the means of execution of the King of the Jews, is part of the liturgy of the day. A cross, usually made of wood, is exposed for the veneration of worshipers. They approach the cross and bow before it or kiss it reverently. This ceremony is said to have originated in Jerusalem, with the object of worship said to have been the "True Cross," the actual object upon which Jesus himself was crucified. In the fourth century, the Emperor Constantine's mother, Helena, rediscovered the cross in the Holy Land and reclaimed it for her fellow Christians. She built shrines and churches in Jerusalem and throughout Palestine to commemorate Christ's passion and death.

A description of the ceremony (from the old *Catholic Encyclopedia*) in the wake of St. Helena's involvement (in fact, sometime after her death) gives a sense of the dramatic intensity of the moment:

A chair is placed for the Bishop in Golgotha behind the Cross . . . a table covered with a linen cloth is placed before him; the Deacons stand around the table, and a silver gilt casket is brought in, inside which is the wood of the holy Cross. The casket is opened and the wood is taken out, and both the wood of the Cross and the Title are placed upon the table. Now, when it has been put upon the table, the Bishop, as he sits, holds the extremities of the sacred wood firmly in his hands, while the Deacons stand around and guard it. It is guarded thus because the custom is that the people, both faithful and catechumens, come one by one and, bowing down at the table, kiss the sacred wood and pass on.

In those days and for more than a millennium after, the celebrant (priest or bishop) wore vestments of black, as he would at a funeral Mass.

To this day, tens of thousands of pilgrims each Good Friday walk the so-called Via Dolorosa (the "Way of Sorrows") to re-create Jesus' carrying the cross to Golgotha, the site of his execution. The Stations of the Cross are prayed in parish churches throughout Holy Week, including Friday evening.

Remember, too, that it is a day of fasting and abstinence, with the faithful required to partake of only one modest meal and no meat. Hot cross buns are an English tradition and are eaten on Good Friday. Some scholars believe that hot buns, minus the cross, first appeared during the pagan spring festivals. Later, monks took the recipe and added the cross as a sign of Christianity.

During medieval times, the crosses on the buns served two purposes. First, they kept the buns fresh for a year or more (serving as a preservative glaze), and second, and perhaps more important, they served to ward off the devil. This superstition was so ingrained that when King Henry VIII broke away from the Church and outlawed the buns, people continued to eat them for fear that the devil would come and get them.

Another English legend tells why the hot cross buns became a tradition of Good Friday. A widow living on the east end of London had an only son who was at sea. Since originally the buns were made at the beginning of Lent, she put one aside for him on Good Friday, for when he returned. The following year, still awaiting his return, she put another bun aside. Every year after, she would put one aside for the boy-who-never-returned. Others translated this little ritual into a sign that called for the resurrected Christ.

On Holy Saturday in some European countries, all candles in the churches are extinguished. That evening, Easter bonfires are lit using only flint. This is known as the "new fire," which is used to relight the candles in the church. People bring charred sticks home from the fire and build their own fire. Then they pray that the home will be protected from fire, lightning, and hail. In Bavaria, wood or straw figures are burned in the fire in a ritual called "the burning of Judas," the Apostle who betrayed Jesus to the authorities on the eve of his crucifixion. In rural areas of Holland, young boys chase young girls around the fire and throw soot on them for good luck. This is believed to be derived from an ancient fertility rite.

It is also believed that the fires are related to an ancient ritual of lighting fires on mountaintops on the spring equinox in order to drive away the darkness of winter.

HOLY SATURDAY AND THE VIGIL OF EASTER

Also called the Angelic Night, Holy Saturday lies between the most solemn solemnity of Good Friday and the highest, holiest, and most exultant day of them all. As of sunset, the fasting of the previous Lenten season is done, and a new season—and for Christians, a new life—begins.

Fire, the reliable old pagan symbol transmuted to new purposes by a new faith, is lit at sunset to begin the liturgy of the Mass. The lighting of lamps and candles during the vigil, in addition to the opening fire, draws attention to the first lighting of the new Paschal candle. This candle will then stand in the sanctuary of the church near the altar and be lit every Sunday for the duration of the Easter season.

This is a time of transition—the prayers of the Alleluia and the Gloria are reinstituted in the Mass from this time forward. One of the most significant and moving elements of the Easter vigil is the reception into the fullness of the faith of the catechumens, adults who have been preparing for baptism and membership in the Church. The chrism, or holy oil, that was presented two nights earlier, at the Holy Thursday liturgy, is used to anoint the candidates during the baptism as a sacrament of initiation.

APRIL FOOLS' DAY

The origin of April Fools' Day has officially been declared "undetermined" by such reliable contemporary websites as snopes.com, and its true origin might never be known for certain. However, all sources commonly acknowledge at least one theory.

According to the old Julian calendar, the new year began on March 25, following the vernal equinox, and the official celebration of the new year fell on April 1. Because the prior week was Holy Week, it took precedence over this lesser civil festival.

In 1563, France's King Charles IX decreed that the new year would begin on January 1, which was codified in Pope Gregory XIII's new calendar, promulgated in 1584, along with a radical reorientation of the entire year.

It was said that, first in France, then in England, and later in other European countries, neighbors tried to trick their more gullible or change-resistant brethren into believing that April 1 was still the new year—thus "fooling" them. The task of doing so was called a "fool's errand."

It is also called All Fools' Day, in a possible swipe at the solemn remembrance on November 1, known as All Saints' Day.

CHAPTER 7

EASTER SUNDAY AND SEASON

Welcome to a new world! On Easter Sunday morning, in nearly every corner of the world, Christians fill parish churches and cathedrals to celebrate the central moment and ultimate manifestation of their faith: The resurrection of Jesus Christ. The concept of the resurrection of the human body lies at the heart of the Christian belief system.

The evangelist Luke, as usual, provides the most compelling narrative of the Easter event (24:1–12):

On the first day of the week, very early in the morning, the women took the spices they had prepared and went to the tomb. They found the stone rolled away from the tomb, but when they entered, they did not find the body of the Lord Jesus.

While they were wondering about this, suddenly two men in
clothes that gleamed like lightning stood beside them. In their
fright the women bowed down with their faces to the ground, but
the men said to them, "Why do you look for the living among the
dead? He is not here; he has risen! Remember how he told you,
while he was still with you in Galilee: 'The Son of Man must be
delivered into the hands of sinful men, be crucified and on the
third day be raised again.'" Then they remembered his words.

When they came back from the tomb, they told all these
things to the Eleven and to all the others. It was Mary Magda-
lene, Joanna, Mary the mother of James, and the others with
them who told this to the apostles. But they did not believe the
women, because their words seemed to them like nonsense.

Peter, however, got up and ran to the tomb. Bending over,
he saw the strips of linen lying by themselves, and he went away,
wondering to himself what had happened.

On this day, after the preparation of the previous seven
weeks, joy and optimism are unleashed within individuals
and the community as a whole. The *festum festorum,* or "feast
of feasts," is the oldest one in the Church, a religious cor-
nerstone, a link to the Jewish tradition from which the faith
was born, as well as the history of the world in which it
"grew up" over two millennia.

The British cleric and historian known as the Venerable
Bede, one of the most reliable sources for the early history
of the Church in Europe, ties the English word "Easter" to

the Germanic goddess of the rising light of day and spring known as "Estre." According to the old *Catholic Encyclopedia* the etymology includes the Anglo-Saxon *eâster* or *eâstron,* in Old High German *ôstra,* and in German *Ostern.*

Controversies and confusions over the dating of Easter have been recounted in books and were the subject of papal declarations and schisms for several centuries. In the Christian West, the date has been fixed loosely around the Jewish feast of Passover, the 14th day of the month Nisan, but not *on* that exact date. Rather, as described in the *Catholic Encyclopedia:* "Easter was celebrated in Rome and Alexandria on the first Sunday after the first full moon after the spring equinox [in the northern hemisphere], and the Roman Church claimed for this observance the authority of Sts. Peter and Paul." Easter has thus become the quintessential celebration of spring, the season of blossoming life, rebirth, and emergence from the dark hibernation of winter.

Those who wanted to fix Easter on a particular day—the day after 14 Nisan in the Jewish calendar—were called Quartodecimans and excommunicated from the Church when the Council of Nicaea in A.D. 325 decreed that the Roman practice should be observed universally. Therefore, Easter, unlike Christmas (on December 25), is a "moveable feast."

While every Sunday of the year is a commemoration of the Savior's resurrection (after all, the event occurred on a Sunday), Easter remains the summit of all memorials and celebrations, elevated by popes and councils, as well as the practice of the faithful everywhere throughout the Church.

Remember the catechumens who were baptized at the Easter Vigil? They are now called neophytes, and they enter a period of their conversion called "mystagogy"—a further instruction and initiation into the mysteries of the faith, which include the Eucharist, the sacrament of confirmation, community, and resurrection. They serve as models to the congregation of the power of faith.

The liturgy of Easter is closely connected to the rite of baptism, which itself symbolizes a dying and rising to new life of the baptized through immersion in water. Throughout the season of Easter, the priest sprinkles the congregation with water, and hymns are sung to remind all the faithful of their own commitment through baptism.

But what about the traditions surrounding Easter: the Easter parade, Easter egg hunts, rabbits, and baskets full of candy? Did Jesus color eggs or eat chocolate bunnies? It's these traditions that may cause people to wonder, as Peter did when Jesus' tomb was found to be empty: *What happened?*

For many of the current Easter traditions, there are different explanations—some based in Christianity and some not. Christians adopted the name "Easter" to make it more comfortable for pagans to become Christians. Druids and other pagans believed that the spring equinox was when the sun god would marry the maiden goddess who would become the Great Mother nine months later. This would coincide with the time of Easter, after the equinox, and the message of Easter became new life.

So what about the eggs? How do they connect to Easter? There's no shortage of explanations. In the pagan tradition, eggs are a celebration of fertility and new life. They were part of the ritual surrounding the celebration of spring, when rebirth occurred. The egg, in some traditions, is the explanation for the universe. Certain Eastern religions, including Hinduism, hold that the earth was created when a giant egg burst. Easter eggs are, in the West, simply an extension of the pagan rituals.

Some believe that the Easter egg symbolizes Jesus' Last Supper, since an egg is a part of a Passover Seder meal. Yet another explanation for Easter eggs comes from England. In medieval times, an Easter tax was due to the Church. Those in rural areas had little money, so they paid the tax in baskets of eggs.

There is another old legend in France that says if you don't eat an egg on Easter, you will be bitten by snakes in the coming year. In England, eggs were blessed by priests and then eaten in thanksgiving for the resurrection of Jesus. In Russia, Easter eggs are believed to have magical powers, ensuring good crops and driving away evil spirits. They are sometimes hidden in the foundations of homes for good luck.

So what about the practice of coloring eggs? Much like the explanations for the origin of the Easter egg, there are many theories about why they are colored. One is that they were forbidden by Church law during Lent, so people colored them to mark the end of the fasting period and eat them at the Easter celebration.

Some scholars think coloring began with the ancient spring festival of Nowruz, which is the Persian new year. Because eggs are life-giving, ancient people did not know whether good or evil would emerge. To exert some kind of control over the power, they would paint signs and symbols with positive connotations or dye the egg red for good luck. The ancient pagans colored eggs to bring joy or to celebrate the bright colors that would come with spring.

The Polish decorate eggs red, blue, and green, in acknowledgment of the legend that Mary, the mother of God, painted eggs these colors to entertain the baby Jesus. Another legend tells of a saint who was called before a Roman emperor. The emperor denied Jesus' resurrection, and the saint pointed to an egg that God had changed into a colored egg as proof.

Egg-coloring may also have begun with early Christians hiding in the catacombs. These men and women, afraid for their lives, painted eggs red to imitate the blood of Christ. Armenians decorate eggs with pictures of Jesus, Mary, and other religious symbols. Austrians fasten ferns and other plants to eggs before boiling them, leaving a design when the egg cools.

Perhaps the most famous and valuable Easter eggs were created by the Russian jeweler Fabergé for Tsars Alexander III and Nicholas II, starting in 1885. These fabulous gifts came in all sizes (some could be worn around the neck) and were decorated with enamel panels, precious metals, and gems. Tsar Nicholas II was overthrown in 1917 and the House of Fabergé was later nationalized by the Bolsheviks, ending generations of this lavish Easter tradition.

Unsurprisingly, considering they invented the Christmas tree, Germans also began the tradition of the Easter egg tree. A stick is used to poke a hole in an egg and drain its contents. The eggs are then colored and hung on a branch using the drainage hole.

THE EASTER RABBIT

The ancient Egyptians believed that the hare was a sign of the moon. The timing of Easter depends on the moon, and there is a legend throughout Europe that says the "white bunny of the moon" brings children Easter eggs.

In Teutonic mythology there is a story that seems to account for the Easter bunny, the Easter egg, and the coloring of Easter eggs. A little girl found a dying bird and prayed to the goddess Eostra. Eostra appeared on a rainbow bridge and, in an apparent attempt to save the badly wounded bird, turned it into a hare. The goddess then told the little girl the hare would return each year, bringing rainbow-colored eggs.

It is in Germany, in 1680, that the first written story about a bunny hiding eggs in a garden appears. When Germans settled in Pennsylvania and became known as the Pennsylvania Dutch, they continued to expand upon the traditions. The bunny became known as Oschter Haws in the 1680s, and children in Germantown began building nests for the bunnies in hats and bonnets, which eventually evolved into baskets.

Germans are very much involved in the lore of, and in creating, many of the traditions surrounding Easter. The first edible bunnies were made in Germany in the nineteenth century and were pastries. In the early twentieth century, the Easter Bunny caught on, and when the song "Peter Cottontail" was written, the Easter Bunny hit the big time.

In the Czech Republic, girls color Easter eggs while boys make *pomlazka,* or Easter whips, out of willow branches and colored ribbons. These are used to symbolically whip the girls on Easter Monday in order to drive away age and preserve their beauty.

A similar ritual is observed in Sweden. Twigs of birch or willow are decorated with colored feathers and ornaments. This tradition is derived from an ancient Swedish tradition, no longer widely practiced, called "Easter Fright." On Good Friday, parents and masters would strike their children and servants with twigs so as to impress upon them the suffering of Jesus Christ during his Passion and death. It was also believed that those who were struck on Good Friday would be obedient for the remainder of the year.

Another theory about the origin of the twigs is that they replaced the palms of Palm Sunday. Immediately following the Reformation, explicitly "Catholic" rituals now considered corrupt were banned in many Protestant countries. Instead of using palms, twigs were blessed and brought into people's homes. Some believe that this tradition may have roots beyond Christianity, as a way for the ancients to transfer the power of growth and life from the twigs to the recipient of the whipping, assuring good health and protection from evil. Today, the Easter twig tradition is dying out, replaced largely by a new tradition, the Easter tree, which is similar to the Christmas tree.

FLOWERS AND OTHER TRADITIONS

Another Swedish Easter tradition is that of young girls dressing as "Easter Witches," and going from door to door collecting candy. This tradition has dubious roots in witch hunts of the Middle Ages.

The Easter lily is a flower that represents spring and is one of the more beautiful symbols of the season. It seems its Easter connections are solely in the Christian tradition.

Lilies are a biblical flower, as noted in Luke 12:27: "Consider the lilies of the field, how they grow: they toil not, neither do they spin; and yet . . . Solomon in all his glory was not arrayed like one of these." As the Easter flower, the bulb in the ground represents Jesus' tomb, and the blossoming flower and its fragrance represent the resurrection. The smooth white appearance represents the purity of Jesus and the joy of the resurrection.

Easter lilies are often referred to as "white-robed apostles of hope," and are said to have grown in Gethsemane following Christ's Agony in the Garden. It is believed that his sweat, blood, and tears during this time were responsible for the flower's growth.

There are many games surrounding Easter. Romans celebrated Easter by running races on oval tracks, with eggs as the prize. According to the Pennsylvania Dutch custom, hiding an egg in a house on Good Friday was supposed to keep lightning from hitting the home. Perhaps these are the traditions that lead to the Easter egg hunt. Another explanation for the Easter egg hunt comes from Germany, where it is said that a woman who lived in times of great famine hid colored eggs for her children in a nest. When she went to retrieve them, she saw a bunny hopping away.

The Easter egg roll probably began in England, in imitation of Christ rolling the stone away from his tomb. The White House Easter Egg roll dates back to 1878. In years prior, beginning with the Madison administration, children gathered at the Capitol on Easter Monday and rolled eggs down the hill. However, following the Easter of 1876, Congress passed the Turf Protection Act, which forbade the use of the Capitol grounds for "recreational use." In 1877, notices appeared in the newspapers just before Easter warning that a large force would be at the Capitol to enforce the new law. Those who showed up that year were turned away.

The following year, President Rutherford B. Hayes reinstated the tradition. There are two accounts of how this occurred. One has a mob of angry youngsters storming the White House gates, eggs in hand, demanding to be let in. The other account is that of a young boy who approached the president on his daily stroll just before Easter and called out to him, "Say! Say! Are you going to let us roll eggs in your yard?" a contemporary newspaper reported the boy asking. President Hayes agreed to look into the matter and, upon consulting with his White House staff, instructed them to allow any children who came by Monday morning access to the South Lawn.

The tradition from which the Easter parade and Easter bonnets come is the wearing of new clothes on Easter. It was thought that to do this would bring good luck. The Easter parade began as an informal gathering in the nineteenth century in New York City. Originally a way to celebrate the tradition of having new clothes, it began as an informal walk down Fifth Avenue. Over the years, the parade grew but remained informal.

In Eastern Europe, families brought their Easter meal to Church to be blessed on Easter day. The meal was carried in a basket; thus the Easter basket was born. According to Gould, "In true Polish tradition, at Easter time, a family Easter basket is prepared. With much love and care, the Easter basket is filled with foods that will be served on Easter Sunday."

The Easter meal is full of religious symbolism. A round loaf of bread is marked with a cross. This tasty bread symbolizes Jesus on the cross and also being the Bread of Life. Those who break the bread receive the Eucharist into their home. Butter is molded into a Paschal Lamb. A red-and-white cross-emblazoned banner decorates the lamb. And what would Easter be without an egg? Colored eggshells refer to the tomb of Christ, while the yellow yoke stands for the radiant sun. Deliciously prepared is Easter ham, along with sausage rings. The ham is a symbol of the Paschal sacrifice. Rings of kielbasa denote unity within a family.

Christ's bitter sufferings are felt by all. Vinegar, pepper, and horseradish are a realistic addition to the basket of Easter foods. Often, ground beets are added to the horseradish. This makes one think of the blood that Jesus shed when he hung on the cross.

Wine is often found in the basket of overflowing goodness. In the Bible, the Psalms encourage the use of wine. Wine gladdens the heart. A glass of wine is the fullness of joy at the Lord's Eucharistic table. Salt preserves that which is good. In fact, the expression, "To eat a barrel of salt with someone" is the same as being someone's best friend.

Meredith Gould notes in *The Catholic Home*, "Numerous desserts add sweetness to the basket. Made with yeast, they symbolize the springtime sun and Jesus rising from the tomb. Another welcome to the return of spring is the Polish palm, or the pussy willow. White depicts the brilliance of the Resurrection, so a pure white doily or cloth covers the Easter basket and it is brought to church for a blessing."

A rather dangerous tradition occurs on Good Friday in the Philippines. Many self-flagellate, imitating the whippings Christ endured during his Passion. Some go as far as being nailed to the cross in a reenactment of Christ's crucifixion.

In pre-communist Russia, there was a custom that anyone who wished could ring the church bell on Easter Day. When people passed, one would say, "Christ is risen," and the other would reply, "He has risen indeed."

There is also a belief around the world that on Easter morning, the sun dances, rejoicing at the resurrection. For this reason, many people on all continents watch the sun rise on Easter morning. This ritual is believed to have been the origin of the sunrise service on Easter.

The first sunrise service in the United States took place in the Moravian Church in Bethlehem, Pennsylvania—a tradition that continues today. Just before sunrise, parishioners, clergy, singers, and the trombone choir leave the church for the cemetery, where they sing a traditional hymn and play the trombones as the sun rises.

CHAPTER 8

MOTHER'S DAY AND THE MONTH OF MARY

May is the month of mothers. In both Church and society at large, it is a month of femininity, a continuation of the Easter theme of fertility. The place of Mary in the Church and its calendar is unassailable. Second only to her son, she is honored with various festivals and holidays that draw Christians' attention to her special place at his side and at the head of the Church.

She is Mother of Christ and Mother of the Church. She is *Theotokos,* the "God-bearer," and Queen of Heaven. She appears at many key points throughout the Gospel narratives, and even in the Acts of the Apostles, after Jesus' death and resurrection. Perhaps one of the most moving moments is her role during the Passion (Christ's suffering),

as the Second Vatican Council explained in the Dogmatic
Constitution on the Church, known as *Lumen gentium:*

> *Thus the Blessed Virgin advanced in her pilgrimage of faith, and*
> *faithfully preserved in her union with her Son unto the cross.*
> *There she stood, in keeping with the divine plan, enduring with*
> *her only begotten Son the intensity of his suffering, joining her-*
> *self with his sacrifice in her mother's heart, and lovingly con-*
> *senting to the immolation of this victim, born of her: to be given*
> *by the same Christ Jesus dying on the cross, as a mother to his dis-*
> *ciple, with these words [from John 19:26–27]: "Woman, behold*
> *your son."*

Mary is the example of "cooperation" with the will of
God, an extreme case of one who said yes to her Lord and
who serves as a model for all women—and men. Special devotions, such as the Rosary and novenas, are offered to her
to ask for her intercession in our lives. And other prayers to
the Mother of Christ are sprinkled throughout the liturgy
and in the daily worship practices of Catholics. Two familiar
examples are these:

The Magnificat (or Canticle of Mary)
My soul does magnify the Lord.
And my spirit has rejoiced in God my Savior.
Because he has regarded the humility of his handmaid;
for behold from henceforth all generations shall call me blessed.

Because he that is mighty,

has done great things for me;

and holy is his name.

And his mercy is from generation unto generations,

To them that fear him.

He has showed might in his arm:

he has scattered the proud in the conceit of their heart.

He has filled the hungry with good things:

and the rich he has sent empty away.

He has received Israel his servant, being mindful of his mercy.

As he spoke to our fathers: to Abraham and to his seed forever.

The Hail Mary

Hail Mary, full of grace, the Lord is with you; blessed are you among women, and blessed is the fruit of your womb, Jesus. Holy Mary, Mother of God, pray for us sinners, now and at the hour of our death. Amen.

May is dedicated by the Church to Mary, the Blessed Virgin. The celebration starts with the Crowning of Mary, on the first or early in May. While placing a crown of flowers on a statue of Mary, children sing: "O Mary, we crown thee with blossoms today, Queen of the Angels, Queen of the May."

May celebrations continue with Mother's Day, held on the second Sunday of the month, which ends with the Feast of the Visitation on May 31. According to Scripture, the

Archangel Gabriel told Mary to visit her cousin Elizabeth, who had been barren but was now with child—a child who would become John the Baptist. When Elizabeth saw Mary, it is reported that she said: "Blessed are you among women, and blessed is the fruit of your womb! And why is this granted me, that the mother of my Lord should come to me?" It is this quote from which the *Hail Mary* is drawn. When these words were spoken to her, Mary supposedly responded with the words of the *Magnificat.*

It's appropriate that the beautiful month of May, the glorious time of spring flowers and nature's awakening, is when we honor the purity and love of the Mother of God along with the purity and love of our own mothers who gave us life.

Mary gave Jesus to the world. He is God-made-man who came to earth to free us from original sin and show us the great love of God. The Bible tells us that Gabriel appeared to Mary and told her that she was to be the virgin mother of God, and Mary said to him: "From this time forth, all generations shall call me blessed."

Mary didn't question God's will; she accepted the holy miracle that was given to her and Joseph, her betrothed, who also believed the angel who appeared to tell him the news. Hence she is revered for her absolute obedience, as strange and difficult as it must have seemed to her, a teenage, unmarried virgin who suddenly was expecting a child.

From that moment on, Mary's life was devoted to her son, and so devotion is what we in turn give to Mary and to all mothers who love their children unconditionally. The story of Mary and the example of Mother Mary is one that helps to elevate motherhood to a blessed status. Good mothers want only the best for their children and will give everything they have for them. This was certainly Mary's example, which the Church highlights at every opportunity.

MOTHER'S DAY

The holiday known as Mother's Day, as we celebrate it today, was suggested by Julia Ward Howe, author of "The Battle Hymn of the Republic," in her "Mother's Day Proclamation," written in 1870. Then, in the early 1900s, Anna Jarvis of Maine worked tirelessly to create a national holiday for mothers. As a result of her efforts, the first Mother's Day was celebrated on May 10, 1908, in Grafton, Pennsylvania, and in Philadelphia at the Methodist churches. In 1912, Jarvis trademarked the phrases "second Sunday in May" and "Mother's Day," and she created the Mother's Day International Association. President Woodrow Wilson declared Mother's Day a national holiday on May 9, 1914.

An early tradition for Mother's Day was to wear a carnation—a colored carnation if your mother was alive, and a white one to remember mothers who were deceased. Today mothers receive flowers and plants on their special day, along with breakfast in bed or dinner out as a family, and other gifts of love.

Today in the United States, Mother's Day produces $1.9 billion in flower sales, $2.9 billion in restaurant tabs, and according to a CBS News story from May 9, 2010, Mother's Day creates the highest call volume of the year (approximately 10 percent higher than St. Valentine's Day).

CHART OF THE FEAST DAYS
OF THE BLESSED VIRGIN MARY

January 1	Solemnity of Mary, Mother of God
	Mary honored as "Theotokos," the mother of God; Jesus' circumcision and naming on octave of his birth
	Holy day of obligation in the United States and Latin America
February 11	Feast of the Apparition of Our Lady at Lourdes
	In 1858, Mary appeared to St. Bernadette Soubirous at Lourdes, France, now a popular healing site.
March 25	Solemnity of the Annunciation of Our Lord to the Blessed Virgin Mary
	Nine months before Christmas commemorates the visit of Archangel Gabriel to the virgin to announce her motherhood of Christ.
May 1	"May Day," the month of crowning of the Queen of Heaven begins

	During this month, local churches, schools, and Rosary Societies hold crownings of statues of the Virgin.
May 13	Memorial of Our Lady of Fatima
	In 1917, Mary appeared to three children at Fatima, Portugal, and revealed three prophecies to them.
May 27	Feast of the Immaculate Heart of Mary
May 31	Feast of the Visitation of the Virgin Mary to Her Cousin Elizabeth
	Commemorates the meeting of cousins Jesus and John the Baptist, each in the womb of his mother.
July 16	Feast of Our Lady of Mount Carmel
	Commemorates the vision from Mount Carmel of the mother of the Savior on a cloud.
	Patron of the Carmelite religious order.
August 5	Memorial of the Dedication of the Basilica of St. Mary Major (or Mary of the Snow)
	A church was built in honor of the Blessed Virgin in fourth-century Rome where snow fell in summertime.
August 15	Solemnity of the Assumption of the Blessed Virgin Mary
	In 1950 Pope Pius XII declared the Catholic doctrine that Mary was assumed bodily into heaven.
	Holy day of obligation.
August 22	Memorial of the Queenship of the Virgin Mary
	Today, the Church teaches that the Blessed Virgin Mary reigns as the Queen of Heaven.
	The octave of the Assumption.

September 8	Feast of the Birthday of the Blessed Virgin Mary
	On the anniversary of the dedication of a church to her mother, Mary's birth is commemorated.
September 12	Memorial of the Holy Name of Mary (optional)
	Starting in Spain in the sixteenth century, the memorial became a universal Church observance in 1863.
September 15	Memorial of Our Lady of Sorrows (or Our Lady of the Seven Sorrows)
	Remembering her sufferings at the foot of the cross and the sword of sorrow that pierced her heart.
October 7	Memorial of Our Lady of the Rosary
	An optional observance that honors the popular prayer to the Blessed Virgin Mary, the Rosary.
October 11	Feast of the Motherhood of Our Lady
	Another feast not as frequently observed, overshadowed by other national Marian feasts.
November 21	Memorial of the Presentation of the Blessed Virgin Mary
	The anniversary of the dedication of a basilica in Jerusalem, honoring her presentation in the temple.
	In Latin America, a patronal feast in several countries.
December 8	Solemnity of the Immaculate Conception of the Blessed Virgin Mary
	In 1854, Pope Pius IX proclaimed the dogma that Mary was conceived free from Original Sin.
	Patron of the United States. Holy day of obligation.

December 12   Feast of Our Lady of Guadalupe

Mary appeared to the Indian, St. Juan Diego, in Tebeynac, Mexico, in 1531.

Patron of the Americas and of Mexico.

ST. JOAN OF ARC

As the month of May begins with the focus on a woman, so it ends, on May 30, with a memorial to one of the most remarkable women in the history of Christianity: St. Joan of Arc, the Maid of Orléans.

Jeanne D'Arc was born into a pious Catholic family in the village of Domrémy in Champagne, France, on January 6, 1412. She died a mere 19 years later on May 30, 1431, in enemy captivity in Rouen, burned at the stake for heresy, sorcery, and adultery. Two decades after her death, in 1455, Pope Callistus III found her innocent of the charges for which she had been condemned, declaring her a martyr for her faith. And she was canonized a saint of the same Church that had condemned her in 1920.

What a journey Joan had, through legend and history, in her very short life. Her image as a warrior for France, a quintessential Catholic nation, is familiar around the world, among both Catholics and non-Catholics: a teenage heroine in soldier's armor, carrying the banner of her king.

It was at age 13, in the summer of 1425, that she first heard the voices that would guide her actions over the last third of her life. According to the *Catholic Encyclopedia*:

> It was at first simply a voice, as if someone had spoken quite
> close to her, but it seems also clear that a blaze of light ac-
> companied it, and that later on she clearly discerned in some
> way the appearance of those who spoke to her, recognizing

them individually as St. Michael [the Archangel] (who was accompanied by other angels), St. Margaret, St. Catherine, and others. Joan was always reluctant to speak of her voices. She said nothing about them to her confessor, and constantly refused, at her trial, to be inveigled into descriptions of the appearance of the saints and to explain how she recognized them. Nonetheless, she told her judges: "I saw them with these very eyes, as well as I see you."

By the time she was 17, after counseling the as yet uncrowned King Charles VII and facing the heavy opposition of experienced courtiers and entrenched churchmen, Joan was given command of an army, which she then led to victory over the English at the besieged city of Orléans on May 8, 1429. "She then enjoyed a series of spectacular military successes, during which the king was able to enter Rheims to be crowned with her at his side."

Joan was captured by the forces of the Duke of Burgundy—ally of the English and enemy of the king of France—at Compiègne in May 1430. For several months she was kept in an iron cage, shackled by the neck, hands, and feet and allowed no spiritual privileges, such as attendance at Mass. Joan was held as a prisoner for a year before she was martyred.

Along with Saints Denis, Martin of Tours, King Louis IX, and Thérèse of Lisieux (also a very young woman at her death), Joan of Arc is a patron saint of France.

THE GREGORIAN CALENDAR

I t's 1582. Take a look at the calendar on your wall. The harvest? You circle the date on the calendar. A wedding? Circle it. And so on. Then, something bizarre shows up. It looks like a terrible misprint. When you get to October, you are shocked to learn that your calendar skips from October 4 to October 15. Eleven days are missing!

Upon further inquiry, you find out that the pope has hit delete on those ten days. The pope! Why?

This is roughly what happened in February 1582. Pope Gregory XIII decreed that by October 1582, the Julian calendar would be replaced by what would come to be called the Gregorian calendar. It is the calendar used around the world today. The Gregorian calendar is accepted—almost universally—for civil and religious purposes. But, as you might suspect, everyone did not immediately accept the change. In fact, it wasn't until the twentieth century that some countries agreed to use the Gregorian calendar. And even today, most Eastern Orthodox churches do not use the calendar to compute when Easter is celebrated each year. And that was the crux of this whole calendar upheaval: when to celebrate Easter.

To understand the history of the Gregorian calendar, let's go back to the early Church. In the Church's first few centuries there were conflicting views about when to celebrate Easter, a pivotal feast of the Christian faith community. What sounds at first like a trivial argument about which day to celebrate Easter is upon closer scrutiny a matter of considerable importance, sparking a centuries-old dispute among theologians called the Quartodecimian Controversy.

At the same time, Christians wanted the timing of the Easter celebration to correspond with biblical accounts. If a passage from Scripture made a particular time reference, the Church Fathers wanted to honor that. A simple example: if believers hold that Jesus Christ died on Good Friday and rose on the third day, wasn't it only fitting that Easter be celebrated each year on a Sunday?

The early Church faced some confusion as to the timing of Easter. Various factions interpreted the date differently. Part of this confusion resulted from not knowing which Gospel to follow (whether the synoptic, Matthew, Mark, and Luke, or the quirkier John); part of it stemmed from the common belief that the Second Coming was imminent anyway. Why be concerned with one date on a calendar?

Other differences involved the interpretations of lunar phases, or when to celebrate the Sabbath.

In A.D. 325, the Emperor Constantine convened the Council of Nicaea (outside modern-day Istanbul) to tackle this controversy, as well as other weighty matters of Christian unity. The result? Rules emerged specifying that Easter should be celebrated on the first Sunday after the first full moon after the vernal equinox, as long as it did not coincide with the beginning of Passover. "By the unanimous judgment of all, it has been decided that the most holy festival of Easter should be everywhere celebrated on one and the same day," Constantine wrote afterward.

To make it easier for the average Christian to know in advance when to mark Easter, special tables were drawn up. But these tables—although they were revised in the following centuries—were imperfect. This was because the Julian calendar, instituted by Julius Caesar in 45 B.C., was off by 11 minutes each year with respect to figuring out the vernal equinox and marking it on a calendar. Under the Julian scheme, the Church used March 21 as the standard for the equinox.

This "drift" does not seem like much, but by A.D. 325, there was already a three-day difference from what was reckoned as the vernal equinox at the time of Caesar. Easter was in danger of falling too late in spring, and it ran the risk of losing its connection to the Jewish Passover.

Fast-forward several hundred years, and we have the Venerable Bede disquieted by the Easter controversy. This scholar knew—as many learned men had known—that the Julian calendar was off-kilter, enough to make a difference in setting the date for Easter as centuries ticked away. As Bede wrote in 731: "It is said that the confusion in those days was such that Easter was sometimes kept twice in one year."

Bede came up with his own calculations of the equinoxes, and is said to have coined the term *catholicus calculator* to describe such a practitioner of *computus,* the Easter timetable calculation.

In this era, factions of Christian Celts and Britons differed by one day on when to celebrate Easter, the Celts having placed the date of Christ's crucifixion on a Thursday by their reading of Scripture. Pope Gregory I dispatched Augustine of Canterbury (not Saint Augustine of Hippo, author of the famous *Confessions*), to settle the dispute. The Synod (local Church council) of Whitby, which took place some 40 miles north of York in 664, has been likened to an "outback" version of Nicaea in 325. At Whitby, the Celts yielded to Rome on when to mark Easter, signifying a victory for Christian unity and a demonstration of the Church's central authority.

Still, although many learned people knew of the flaws of the Julian calendar, it wasn't as if these shortcomings affected the daily life of a peasant, a merchant, or a parish priest. In 1226 another monk, Roger Bacon, again in Britain, possessed such a keen intellect that he intuited the *computus* tables were off. He pushed for reform of the calendar and championed scientific methods. In this account from the *Catholic Encyclopedia*, Bacon acknowledged the superiority of Arab contributions to science and criticized the practice of rounding off numbers with respect to the calendar:

> For the whole order of Church solemnities is thrown into confusion by errors of this kind respecting the beginning of the lunation according to the Calendar, as well as by the error in determining the equinoxes. And not to refer to other years for evidence of this error, I shall state the case in this present year. . . . Wherefore the feast of Easter, by which the world is saved, will not be celebrated at its proper time, but there is fasting this year through the whole true week of Easter. For the fast continues eight days longer than it should. There follows then another disadvantage that the fast of Lent began eight days too late; therefore Christians were eating meats in the true Lent for eight days, which is absurd. And again then neither the Rogations nor the Ascension nor Pentecost are kept this year at their proper times. And as it happens in this year 1267, so it will happen the year following.

In the next several hundred years, several popes attempted to satisfy the goal of "one Easter Sunday for all

Christians" as set by the Council of Nicaea and subsequent synods. In 1344, Pope Clement VI, perhaps partially spurred on by Roger Bacon's findings, solicited expert advice on correcting the calendar. Nothing came of it. It's possible that fighting the Black Plague took precedence at the time. But after the publication of Johannes Gutenberg's Bible in the mid-1400s, the popularity of printed materials skyrocketed, and calendar reform took on some urgency.

Pope Leo X enlisted some professional guidance on the pesky calendar problem. In 1514 he called upon an advocate of calendar reform, Paul of Middleburg, to lead a commission. Paul was a physician, astronomer, and bishop who had campaigned for a series of changes to correct the drift in dates assigned to the vernal equinox, including the use of what tables to calculate the Easter holiday called the Alfonsine Tables, developed in 1272 under the Castilian King Alfonso X.

This reform effort failed when Pope Leo X's letters to Christian leaders were largely ignored. The Church obviously had larger issues to deal with in the sixteenth century, such as the growing Reformation movement.

While no Church leaders responded to Leo's letters, the astronomer Nicolas Copernicus did write back. In fact, Copernicus makes note of Leo X's letter in his dedication to *De revolutionibus*, his great work describing how the earth orbits the sun.

Finally, the Council of Trent in 1563 agreed on reforms of the Roman Catholic breviary (the prayer book for clergy) and Mass book, which opened the door for succeeding popes to reconstruct the calendar in earnest. Thus, Pope Pius V approved minor changes of lunar tables affecting Easter with the stipulation that further drift in the Church's understanding of the vernal equinox be avoided. This was easier said than done, astronomers felt; a more substantial recasting was needed.

Enter Pope Gregory XIII, who succeeded Pius V in 1572 and who was eager to finish the reforms called for by the Council of Trent. One factor in Pope Gregory's enthusiasm for championing change was the Tower of Winds that he had built between 1578 and 1580 in the Vatican. The building housed various state-of-the-art astronomical instruments. Astronomers were able to measure the altitude of the sun at noon through a hole in the wall and chart the differences over the course of seasons as a ray of sunlight projected onto a line. These observations convinced the pope that the equinoxes as specified in the Julian calendar were inaccurate, cementing in his mind the need for reform.

But which approach to reform should Gregory follow?

One method was proposed by Aloysius Lilius, a physician and astronomer. He is the unsung hero of the Gregorian calendar. Lilius proposed a ten-day calendar change to correct the drift since 325. He suggested that it would be possible to implement the change either over the course of 40 years, or even in one fell swoop. In a nutshell, the plan involved having a leap-year day in 97 years out of 400 instead of in one year out of four (as in the Julian calendar). Thus, years divisible by 100 would be leap years, but only if those years were also evenly divisible by 400. As a result, Easter would never occur before March 22, nor later than April 25.

To study this and other proposals, Pope Gregory set up a special commission that included scientists, historians, scholars, and churchmen. In the course of the deliberations, Aloysius Lilius died, but his brother Antonio served on the commission and advocated for his proposal.

Although Aloysius Lilius passed from the scene before the commission had completed its work, his contribution would provide the fundamental solution for calendar reform that would ultimately be adopted. But as with all bureaucracy, before that point could be reached, Pope Gregory, like his predecessors, sought outside opinions. A 20-page compendium of Lilius' proposal was circulated; this time, responses were more forthcoming. In 1580, the commission submitted a report to Pope Gregory. For the most part, it asked the pontiff, who was now almost 80, to implement most of Lilius' ideas. Signers of the report even included an Arabic-speaking patriarch from the Eastern Church.

If Aloysius Lilius was the genius behind the commission's work, then the Jesuit astronomer Christopher Clavius was its chief promoter and tireless defender. Clavius wrote a definitive, 800-page defense of the reform, devoting his life to the cause and writing numerous, carefully argued letters and essays until his death in 1612.

Gregory XIII accepted the findings of his commission on February 24, 1582. A copy of his papal decree was posted on the doors of Saint Peter's Basilica on March 1. The implementation of the changes was set for October 1582. The day after Thursday, October 4, would be Friday, October 15. The vernal equinox of 1583 and all years afterward would fall around March 21. A table of new moons and full moons would be used to compute the date of Easter for each year.

The centuries-long march toward calendar reform was done. Or was it? Would the people accept this Gregorian calendar, any more than we would if our calendar suddenly "lost" ten or eleven days?

Predominantly Catholic countries quickly agreed to use the calendar, though that's not to say that people weren't unruffled. Spain, Portugal, parts of present-day Italy and Holland, Luxemburg, Poland, France, and Belgium adopted the Gregorian calendar, at least in part, as early as 1582. Several regions followed suit in the next several years: including present-day Austria, Germany, Czech Republic, Slovakia, Hungary, and Switzerland. But acceptance or rejection within any country depended heavily on a particular region's allegiance to the Roman Catholic Church or, alternatively, to its embrace of the Protestant Reformation.

Ironies abounded. According to the new calendar, even the birthday of Pope Gregory XIII changed, from January 1, 1502, to January 11, 1502.

Some opponents made extreme claims, with one German theologian asserting that the reform was a ruse intended to make Christians observe holy days on the wrong dates. Michael Maestlin, a prominent opposition astronomer, argued that the pope was taking ten days from people's lives. Another group believed that birds would become confused or that farmers would not know when to plant their crops. On the other end of the spectrum, Catholics in Italy claimed that a tree miraculously blossomed ten days early, thereby validating the pontifical reform.

Stiff resistance lasted for centuries. Many Protestant-majority countries did not adopt the Gregorian calendar until the eighteenth century (for example, parts of Germany, Holland, Norway, Denmark, Switzerland, and Finland). England and its colonies were especially stubborn in their refusal. Despite general approval from Queen Elizabeth I, England, Scotland, Ireland, and the colonies in America held out until 1752. This is why to the present day confusion exists about when to note George Washington's birthday—February 11 or February 22? Accounts at that time often marked dates with "O.S." for Old Style, referring to the Julian calendar, or "N.S." for New Style, referring to the Gregorian calendar. The hodgepodge of acceptance or rejection resulted in eccentricities, such as Sweden having a February 30 in 1712.

Although initiated in 1582, becoming widely accepted as a civil standard by the eighteenth century, the Gregorian calendar did not win acceptance in Greece, Turkey, or Persia until as late as the 1920s. And even today, after all the ardent and passionate efforts of hundreds of years, Constantine's goal still falls short: many Orthodox churches celebrate Easter on a day that either uses the Julian calendar or some variant that causes Easter to fall on a different day from the one accepted by the rest of Christendom.

Today, we live in an age of atomic clocks (which require yearly calibrations of "leap seconds"). We have an international standard (ISO 8601) that seeks to govern the keeping of time. But the shadow of 1582 falls upon us just as surely as each year's vernal equinox.

PART III

SUMMER

From the doldrums to the dog days, summer is the season of holidays on the opposite pole from Christmas (pun intended!): the summer solstice, the longest day of the year versus the winter solstice, the shortest.

The long summer break from school is especially welcome, as are the anticipated American patriotic commemorations such as Memorial Day (the unofficial start of summer), Independence Day on July 4, and Labor Day (the unofficial ending of summer).

Thus, from Father's Day in early June through the reopening of school in September—with family vacations and road trips scheduled long in advance—the supposedly laziest season according to the Christian calendar is often crammed with activities around one holiday or another.

It is a long season that somehow seems to flash by more quickly than anyone would like. Catholics enjoy vacations and public holidays along with everyone else, as well as observing special feast days such as the Solemnity of the Assumption of the Blessed Virgin Mary or the feast of her "birthday." (Was Mary really born on September 8?)

CHAPTER 9

ASCENSION, PENTECOST, AND FATHER'S DAY

The Feast of the Ascension is observed on the fortieth day after Easter Sunday, marking the ascension of Jesus Christ into heaven after his resurrection. It always falls on a Thursday and is, for Catholics, a holy day of obligation, which means mandatory attendance at Mass. The scriptural sources for this feast include the Gospels of Mark 16:19 and Luke 24:51, and this passage from the Acts of the Apostles (1:2–11):

> *He presented himself alive to them by many proofs after he had suffered, appearing to them during forty days and speaking about the kingdom of God. While meeting with them, he enjoined them not to depart from Jerusalem, but to wait for "the promise of the Father*

about which you have heard me speak; for John baptized with water, but in a few days you will be baptized with the Holy Spirit."

When they had gathered together they asked him, "Lord, are you at this time going to restore the kingdom to Israel?"

He answered them, "It is not for you to know the times or seasons that the Father has established by his own authority. But you will receive power when the Holy Spirit comes upon you, and you will be my witnesses in Jerusalem, throughout Judea and Samaria, and to the ends of the earth."

When he had said this, as they were looking on, he was lifted up, and a cloud took him from their sight. While they were looking intently at the sky as he was going, suddenly two men dressed in white garments stood beside them. They said, "Men of Galilee, why are you standing there looking at the sky? This Jesus who has been taken up from you into heaven will return in the same way as you have seen him going into heaven."

All too typically, the Eastern Orthodox tradition and the Western, or Latin, tradition differ on the meaning of the Ascension. In the East, the feast was known as *analepsis*, the "taking up," and as *episozomene*, or the "salvation"—both more passive than the Latin term *ascension*, which means more specifically that Christ raised himself up by his own powers. This is a fine theological point, perhaps, but one of a long list that has separated Eastern and Western Christianity for a millennium.

From that same internal conflict arose the eventual clear separation of Ascension from Pentecost, the commemoration of the descent of the Holy Spirit upon the faithful in Jerusalem, fifty days after Jesus' resurrection. For some centuries in many local churches, the two were celebrated on the same day.

As with Passion and Easter Sundays, as well as Pentecost, the Ascension ranks liturgically among the most solemn in the calendar. It has a vigil and, since the fifteenth century, an octave of preparation with time enough for a novena cycle.

The Feast of the Ascension is one of the earliest in the Christian tradition, dating from the first century, perhaps as early as A.D. 68, within a few years of the martyrdom of the Apostles St. Peter and St. Paul in Rome. Its connection to Easter, as a direct extension of that holiest of holy days, speaks to its prominence and antiquity. Only in the decades since the Second Vatican Council (in the 1960s) has the Ascension seemingly lost some of its urgency in Catholics' observance.

FESTIVITIES

Ascension Day is celebrated in Protestant Germany as Father's Day and is a public holiday, as it is in France and the Netherlands—though not in the United States or the rest of the English-speaking world. In Sweden, it is a bird-watching, or bird-listening, day, with sunrise excursions called *gökotta,* meaning "early cuckoo morning." Hearing a cuckoo directly from the east or the west is considered good luck.

In England, the day is marked with springtime water-based festivals such as "well dressing"—decorating local wells. Other British customs include "beating the Bounds," which entails beating boys with willow branches as they are pushed along parish boundaries not only to purify them of evil but, it is thought, to instruct them about the limits of their parish. This custom is observed in contemporary times by a similar walking tour of farm, church, or town boundaries and may include the planting of a hedge, called a "penny hedge," to mark those borders. Today inanimate objects (not human boys) may be beaten with sticks.

Other customs associated with the feast were the blessing of beans and grapes, the extinction of the Paschal candle for the day, and triumphal processions with torches and banners outside parish churches symbolizing the entry of Christ into heaven. Again in England, where Ascension festivities varied widely, the banner carried at the head of the procession bore the picture of a lion and, at the foot of the banner, a dragon to represent Christ's triumph over the Evil One.

In mountainous central Europe, in Austria and Hungary, one nonliturgical and semi-secular form of celebration includes mountain climbing, in the Alps and elsewhere, to commemorate Christ's ascension into heaven from the Mount of Olives. The universal liturgical color of this feast day is white, for the purity and sinlessness of Christ.

Ten days later, on the 50th day after the celebration of Christ's resurrection on Easter, the Apostles, Mary the mother of Jesus, and other friends and disciples gathered in the city of Jerusalem, where their Savior had been crucified. The occasion was the harvest festival that Jews celebrated on the 50th day of Passover. This event where Mary and friends met is known as Pentecost.

The Pentecost has been described as one of three "megafestivals" in the Christian calendar, along with the better-known and more publicly celebrated holidays of Christmas and Easter. On this day, as described in the Acts of the Apostles (2:1–41) and foretold in the Old Testament, the Holy Spirit was poured out on those gathered in the house as they were praying. A sound much like a roaring wind was heard by those present and the visible sign of tongues of fire descended upon their heads.

These disciples, who were at first frightened by the threat from the Jewish and Roman establishments to their nascent movement, immediately went out into the streets of Jerusalem and began to preach to the crowds there, who were also present for the festival. By a miracle of the power of the Holy Spirit, these followers of Christ spoke of their new faith in the languages of their hearers, in the many foreign tongues heard throughout the Roman Empire.

Peter, the putative leader of the Apostles, seized the moment and became the most visible and most vocal preacher. He proclaimed the Gospel of the death and resurrection of Jesus of Nazareth for the forgiveness of the sins of all mankind.

Thus, Pentecost is regarded, by Catholics especially, as the "birthday" of the Christian Church.

Pentecost has also been commonly termed Whitsunday, from the ancient tradition in which churches used to baptize adult converts to the faith on this day as an alternative to during the Easter Vigil. Those being baptized wore white robes, so it was called "White Sunday." These days, the priest wears red vestments at this feast, signifying the tongues of fire that came down from heaven.

Further, many Catholic dioceses and local parishes confer the sacrament of confirmation on young people on Pentecost Sunday. This rite signifies a coming of age and an acceptance of the fullness of the Christian faith in the same way as a bar or bat mitzvah does in the Jewish tradition.

THE ICE SAINTS

One of the now-obscure but fascinating cycles is that of the so-called Ice Saints, observed in the faith and folklore of Switzerland, the Netherlands, Germany, Austria, Hungary, and Poland. St. Mamertus was a fifth-century bishop of Vienne in Gaul (modern-day France); St. Pancras of Rome was a fourth-century martyr in the persecutions of Diocletian; and St. Servatius was a fourth-century bishop of Maastricht-Tongeren in modern-day Belgium. Their memorials fall on May 11, 12, and 13 respectively, which can often be a time of the return of a brief cold spell in late spring, before the warmth of pre-summer sets in for good.

A spectacular railway terminal in central London, named for St. Pancras and known as the "cathedral of railroad stations," opened in 1868. It featured a beautiful clock tower and soaring public spaces, with a grand hotel across the street designed to complement the Victorian structure. St. Pancras is regarded as the protector against false witnesses and avenger of perjury.

May 14 is the memorial of St. Boniface of Tarsus (the Apostle Paul's original stomping grounds), who died as a martyr around A.D. 306, and who is sometimes included—especially in Poland—as the fourth of the Ice Saints. Then there is St. Sophia, another martyr of the Diocletian period of the early fourth century, who is remembered on May 15 and is the fifth of the Ice Saints. She is sometimes known as "Cold Sophia" or "Wet Sophia" and invoked against the springtime return of cold weather as her icy brethren.

The nights of this period are also sometimes called "iron nights" to denote the same unseasonable return of frost, which, in Sweden and the other Scandinavian countries, may extend into June, even closer to summer.

ST. GEORGE'S DAY

The patron saint and protector of England is St. George, whose memorial is celebrated on April 23. He was adopted as patron by Portugal, by soldiers, and by the Boy Scouts worldwide. His intercession is also invoked by those who pray for a cure from skin diseases.

The image of the legendary, heroic St. George is vivid for most Catholics and others in Western culture: the valiant mounted knight slaying a dragon with his lance. The historical veracity of this saint's life and death has been doubted by some, and his identity has sometimes been confused with other martyrs of the early fourth century.

St. George is thought to have died in Lydda, Palestine, on April 23, A.D. 303, during the persecution of Christians by the emperor Diocletian. A church was erected in his honor there during the reign of the Christian Emperor Constantine. It was later destroyed, and then rebuilt by Crusaders in the eleventh century. That church was razed to the ground by Saladin in the twelfth century, and was later replaced by another in 1872, which still stands today.

Before he was executed by imperial edict for refusing to renounce his Christian faith, George, a high-ranking Roman soldier, gave his considerable wealth to the poor. He was tortured and decapitated. One untitled medieval narrative of his martyrdom, thought to be apocryphal, is particularly gory:

Three times George is put to death—chopped into small pieces, buried deep in the earth, and consumed by fire. But each time, he is resuscitated by the power of God. Besides this we have dead men brought to life to be baptized, wholesale conversions, including that of the Empress Alexandra [and Athanasius, later a bishop], armies and idols destroyed instantaneously, beams of timber suddenly bursting into leaf, and finally milk flowing instead of blood from the martyr's severed head.

After he passed from the scene, a fabulous legend grew up around him, which has defined our vision of him forever. That legend is St. George and the dragon:

A terrible dragon had ravaged all the country near the city of Lydda in Palestine, making its lair in a marshy swamp. Its very breath caused pestilence whenever it approached the town, so the people gave the monster two sheep everyday to satisfy its hunger. But when the sheep no longer satisfied the beast, and a human victim became necessary, lots were drawn among the people to determine who would be sacrificed.

When the lot fell to the daughter of the king, the monarch offered all his wealth to purchase a substitute, but the people had pledged that no substitutes should be allowed, and so the young maiden, dressed as a bride, was led to the dragon's lair.

The Roman soldier, George, happened to ride by and asked the girl what was happening, thinking she had done some wrong and was being punished for it. She bade him leave her, lest he also perish. The valiant knight stayed, however, and when the dragon appeared, St. George made the Sign of the Cross and bravely attacked the beast, skewering it with his lance.

Then he asked the maiden for her girdle and bound it around the neck of the dragon, so that she could lead it back to the city like a lamb. Once they returned, St. George asked the people to be baptized as Christians, then he cut off the dragon's head in their presence. The people did convert, and the king offered the hero half his kingdom. Rather, the knight refused the reward and bade the king to build churches, honor the clergy, and have pity on the poor.

Using the maiden's girdle to tame the dragon links St. George to the patronage of the British Order of the Garter. As per the old edition of the *Catholic Encyclopedia*, his cross became the emblem of England and is still seen in the Union Jack. During the middle ages, April 23 was considered one of the greatest holidays in the Christian calendar of England, almost as festive and important as Christmas.

CATHOLIC MARTYRS OF THE HOLOCAUST
AND THEIR FEAST DAYS

Titus Brandsma: Memorial July 27, beatified November 3, 1985. Born in the Netherlands in 1881, Brandsma joined the Carmelite order and was ordained a priest in 1905. He was a teacher of philosophy, a university rector, and a journalist who fought the spread of Nazism and fascism, urging his fellow Dutch Catholic journalists not to print German propaganda when his country was occupied by Nazi forces. He was arrested in January 1942 and was executed just five months later in Dachau.

Edith Stein: Memorial August 9, canonized October 11, 1998. St. Teresa Benedicta of the Cross is the religious name of Edith Stein. Born into a well-to-do German Jewish family, she became a brilliant scholar and philosopher, converting to Catholicism as an adult. She then entered the Carmelite religious order as a nun. During the darkest days of World War II, she moved to a convent in the Netherlands but was apprehended there by the Gestapo. Edith Stein was murdered at Auschwitz in 1942 at the age of 50 when she would renounce neither her Catholic faith nor her Jewish heritage.

Maximilian Kolbe: Memorial August 14, canonized October 10, 1982. A Polish Franciscan friar, born in 1894, he had been a missionary to Japan and was devoted to the veneration of the Blessed Virgin Mary. After the outbreak of World War II, Kolbe sheltered refugees from the German invaders of his native land, including some two thousand Jews. He was arrested by the Gestapo and sent to a concentration camp, ending up in Auschwitz. It was there that he volunteered to die by lethal injection in place of a stranger, earning him the status of a martyr of the Church.

CHAPTER 10

ORDINARY TIME

The season after Pentecost is the longest season of the liturgical year, lasting from Trinity Sunday through the first Sunday of Advent. This is the non-festival portion of the Church calendar, when it stresses vocation, evangelization, missions, stewardship, almsgiving, and other works of so-called corporal mercy and charity.

For a few weeks in January and February, then all throughout the summer and fall, the Catholic Church is in Ordinary Time. The word "ordinary" comes from the Latin *ordo* meaning "order," and *ordinal,* or *ordinalis,* meaning "counted." Each of the weeks is assigned a number, like the Fourth Sunday in Ordinary time, or the Twentieth Sunday in Ordinary Time.

"Ordinary" does *not* mean ordinary in our contemporary usage of the word: usual or uneventful. Yet there is something rather solid, plodding, and earthy about this long swath of time, nearly six months in all. The themes of the Mass—drawn from the readings—vary from one week to another. And during Ordinary Time, the Gospel readings on Sunday follow Jesus of Nazareth episodically in the books of Matthew, Mark, or Luke. Each of those "synoptic" (similar) Gospels is followed in alternate years or cycles, labeled A, B, and C, so that the entire New Testament is covered over a three-year span.

Also during this time, on Sundays (and at daily Mass), readings are drawn from the letters of St. Paul and others (including St. Peter), which provide both historical and theological dimensions to the liturgy. Readings from the Old Testament are also proclaimed throughout the year, bringing the entire Bible into play—for those who are paying attention!

The use of Ordinary Time was established before the Second Vatican Council, which lasted from 1962 to 1965, but it was not until after the council that the term was officially used to designate the period between Epiphany and Lent, and between Pentecost and Advent. Some Protestant and Anglican denominations still use the older terminology of the "Season after Epiphany" and the "Season after Pentecost," in contradistinction to Catholic usage.

TRINITY SUNDAY

The first Sunday after Pentecost honors the Holy Trinity, one of the most sacred doctrines of the Catholic Church: the teaching that God is three persons in one, the Father, the Son, and the Holy Spirit. This is perhaps the greatest mystery of the Christian faith, that is, something that is unknowable yet irresistible and foundational to belief. In his book, Laurence Hull Stookey writes:

> Orthodox Trinitarian interpretations insist that all three persons exist together from all eternity to all eternity. The Trinity cannot know incompleteness. Trinitarianism is in fact a way of affirming that God *is* completeness, and that all existence proceeds from the fullness of God. This is likely one of the reasons that Trinity Sunday had no general observance in the Western Church until 1334. Indeed, in the 11th century, Pope Alexander II resisted the observance of Trinity Sunday, saying that the Trinity in its fullness is honored on every day of the Church year, and that a discrete observance could serve only to obscure this fact.

Thus, in recapitulating the critical and often-misunderstood concept of the Trinity for the faithful in the pews—calling their attention explicitly to something that is, or should be, a part of the very fabric of Catholic faith—Trinity Sunday becomes a teaching moment and a day for deep reflection. There is no occasion or festive event celebrated on this day. Ordinary Time starts on the Monday after Pentecost.

CORPUS CHRISTI

This familiar-sounding term means "the body and blood of Christ" and is the theme of the following Sunday, the second in Ordinary Time. Corpus Christi is a precious connection—direct, physical, temporal, and eternal—to the person of Jesus Christ. The Solemnity of the Most Holy Body and Blood of Christ is redolent of the high Middle Ages and finds devout observance among the faithful even today.

Eucharistic adoration, a uniquely Catholic ritual, is based on the belief in the "real presence" of Jesus in the consecrated host (the wafer of unleavened bread that is transformed in the Mass into his body—a process called transubstantiation), as well as in the consecrated wine. Catholic churches are required to have a tabernacle—a sacred receptacle—in the sanctuary for the safekeeping of hosts that have not been consumed. These hosts are not disposed of—to practicing Catholics, the substance has been transformed into something new and divine: the actual flesh of Jesus Christ.

So, in order to focus the devotion of the faithful on this central aspect of Catholicism, a consecrated host is sometimes displayed for veneration, either within the church itself or, especially in previous times and cultures, outdoors during a public festival—for example, leading a parade during the observance of a holy day. Think of the street festival portrayed in the film *The Godfather: Part II,* with gaudy lights and images of the Virgin Mary and people standing shoulder to shoulder making the Sign of the Cross.

The monstrance is the vessel in which the Eucharist is placed, visible through a glass window, and which is raised in adoration and blessing at various points during the rite. (In centuries past, the monstrance was also used as a "reliquary" to display the relics of saints.) Most monstrances are made of gold, perhaps silver, with elaborate and intricate designs that surround and call attention to the central display of the Eucharistic object.

Some individual Catholics—and some Catholic parishes—carry this traditional devotion to its ultimate extent with what is called "perpetual adoration." This does not depend on any other occasion or feast, or even hour of the day or day of the week. In fact, it is just what it says: a perpetual, 24/7 adoration of or "keeping watch" over the Blessed Sacrament, often in a chapel dedicated specifically for this purpose. A member of the parish will be present at all times before the tabernacle or the monstrance in a solemn attitude of prayer and reflection on this holiest and most intimate of mysteries.

Continuing the Christological focus of the long period of Ordinary Time—and within the octave of Pentecost—is the Solemnity of the Sacred Heart of Jesus on the third Friday after Pentecost Sunday. The feast first appeared in the universal Church calendar in 1856, during the pontificate of Pius IX, and is thus a comparative newcomer to the list of solemnities, which are, by definition, the major Catholic holy days.

Like Eucharistic adoration, the devotion to the Sacred Heart is woven into the fabric of Catholicism, having developed, primarily within religious congregations such as Benedictines, Franciscans, and Dominicans, in the mid to late Middle Ages. The Jesuits (officially called the Society of Jesus) got on the bandwagon later, in the seventeenth century. Some of the saints devoted to the Sacred Heart of Jesus were Francis de Sales, Aloysius Gonzaga, and Margaret Mary Alacoque. To St. Margaret Mary, a mystical French nun, it is said that Christ revealed the desires of his heart and confided the task of imparting new life to this devotion.

The heart is the emblem of love and the physical engine of life itself. Thus sentiment, religion, mysticism, and even science combine to form an aura around the organ that Jesus, as a human being, possessed, as do we all. Among the five wounds of his crucifixion, the wound in the heart— literally and figuratively—is the most prominent. The heart thus became the traditional source of Franciscan and Jesuit spiritualities.

This devotion is much more individual and personal than public, though images of the Sacred Heart of Jesus are familiar throughout the Catholic world.

Pope John Paul II, who was known for his Marian devotion, instituted the Feast of the Immaculate Heart of Mary as an obligatory observance immediately after Sacred Heart, within the octave of Pentecost.

The Feast of the Transfiguration of the Lord is celebrated on August 6. The transfiguration was a manifestation of Jesus' divinity, witnessed by the Apostles Peter, James, and John on a mountaintop apart from the other disciples. It was a climax of a sort of his public ministry, recounted in detail in the Gospels of Matthew (17:1–6), Mark (9:1–9), and Luke (9:28–36). Here is Mark's account of the astounding event:

After six days, Jesus took Peter, James, and John and led them up a high mountain apart by themselves. And he was transfigured before them, and his clothes became dazzling white, such as no fuller on earth could bleach them. Then Elijah appeared to them, along with Moses and they were conversing with Jesus.

Then Peter said to Jesus in reply, "Rabbi, it is good that we are here! Let us make three tents: one for you, one for Moses, and one for Elijah." He hardly knew what to say, they were so terrified. Then a cloud came, casting a shadow over them, then from the cloud came a voice, "This is my beloved son. Listen to him." Suddenly, looking around, they no longer saw anyone but Jesus alone with them.

As they were coming down from the mountain, he charged them not to relate what they had seen to anyone, except when the Son of Man had risen from the dead.

The sacred observance was seized upon by political and religious powers when, in celebration of a victory by the Hungarians over the Ottomans at the siege of Belgrade, Pope Callistus III, who received the news on August 6, 1456, proclaimed the Transfiguration a feast to be celebrated by the Universal Church.

The Feast of the Exaltation of the Holy Cross, also known as Holyrood and Roodmas, is held on September 14. It came into existence in Rome toward the end of the seventh century. It spread throughout Christendom as a commemoration of, first, the finding of the True Cross (on which Jesus of Nazareth had been crucified) and, later, the recovery of the cross from the Persians, who had stolen it from Jerusalem. In the earliest days, going back to the fourth century at the time of the dedication of churches and shrines in Jerusalem, it was a holy day of obligation with its own octave which was held among the highest of festivals. According to the *Catholic Encyclopedia*:

> *The most ancient adoration of the cross in the Church is described in the* Ordo Romanus, *generally attributed to St. Gregory [the Great]. It is performed, according to this* Ordo, *just as it is nowadays, after a series of responsory prayers. The cross is prepared before the altar; priests, deacons, subdeacons, clerics of the inferior grades, and lastly the people, each one comes in his turn; they salute the cross, during singing of the anthem,* Ecce lignum crucis in quo salus mundi pependit. Venite adoremus. *Behold*

the wood of the cross on which the salvation of the world did hang. Come let us adore.

The other major adoration of the Holy Cross takes place during the Good Friday liturgy.

Like the Holy Grail, the so-called True Cross has long since passed out of history and into the mists of religious legend and devotion. For many centuries, the idea that the cross upon which Jesus died had survived, and could actually be seen and touched, roused the fevered imagination of Christians. Even today, slivers of wood are venerated as sometimes probable—or merely possible—fragments of the "tree" upon which the Savior hung.

LITURGY OF THE HOURS

In the Catholic tradition, the day has its own rhythms and meanings. The hours of the day are divided into the canonical hours during which priests, deacons, religious, and some lay persons pray from the Breviary, also called the Divine Office (*Officium Divinum*), a comprehensive book of daily prayers for clergy. In some religious communities or parishes, the prayers are sung in unison. At six A.M, noon, and six P.M. the Angelus is prayed, often accompanied by the ringing of the parish church bells.

Some Catholics also pray, instead of or in addition to the above, the morning offering upon awakening, and they might make a nightly examination of conscience just before retiring for the day.

Jews, Greeks, and Romans historically divided the hours between sunrise and sunset into 12 parts of roughly one hour in length. The Jews devoted some of those intervals to prayer, as did Christians who followed them in the biblical tradition. This is noted in both Old and New Testaments. For example:

> *Evening and morning, and at noon, I will speak and declare; and he shall hear my voice.*
>
> —*Psalm 54:17*

> *Now Peter and John went up into the temple at the ninth hour of prayer.*
>
> —*Acts 3:1*

Clergy are obligated to say the prayers of the Office. At least some are and should be said publicly in churches, especially Matins and Vespers.

Vigils: Prayers offered during evening "watches," four times at three-hour intervals

Matins: The sunrise office that may contain three nocturnes from previous vigils

Lauds: Meaning "praises," offered as morning prayer, also at sunrise

Prime: Once offered at six A.M., the "prime hour," now abolished

Terce: At nine A.M., or the third hour

Sext: At noon, or the sixth hour; Prime, Terce, and Sext collectively known as the "Little Hours"

None: At three P.M. or the ninth hour

Vespers: Evening prayer, also known as "evensong" and often sung

Compline: Night prayer, prayed after sunset, before bed

CHAPTER 11

SACRED AND
SECULAR SUMMER
HOLIDAYS

In the United States, Memorial Day is a near-perfect blending of sacred meaning and secular celebration, with a patriotic purpose. It is the unofficial beginning of the summer season in the Northern Hemisphere. Originally called "Decoration Day" when first proclaimed by General John A. Logan, national commander of the Grand Army of the Republic for May 30, 1868, it was deemed a day to place flowers on the graves of soldiers buried in Arlington National Cemetery—both Union and Confederate.

A Congressional resolution passed in 2000 asks that, at three P.M. local time, all Americans "voluntarily and informally observe in their own way a moment of remembrance and respect [for U.S. servicemen and women who have fallen in wartime], pausing from whatever they are doing for a moment of silence or listening to 'Taps.'" Since 1971 Memorial Day has been observed on the last Monday in May.

HOMO LUDENS

Summer is the time for the human spirit to mark time. In modern Western society it is a time reserved for *homo ludens*, or playing man, the part of human beings that seeks leisure and respite from work and responsibility. In America, such time is scarce in comparison to, say, European society—Europeans generally have more vacation time than their American counterparts. Nevertheless, time reserved for vacations and recreation permits the spirit to be refreshed, much as it did for Jesus and his disciples when they went off far from the public eye near the village of Ephraim (John 7:1; John 11:54). Throughout the Gospel accounts, Christ and his followers retreat, sometimes together, sometimes separately, to pray and rest from the demands of his ministry.

Summer also offers us ample time for several notable secular holidays. These observances are modeled on the well-established religious concept of the day set apart for commemoration and celebration. One such date is Flag Day, celebrated on June 14. That particular day was selected because on June 14, 1777, the Continental Congress approved the design of a national flag.

However, before Flag Day achieved official status as a holiday it had been celebrated in various locales for many years, especially by schoolchildren. Some reports say a Wisconsin teacher in 1885 had begun the observance of a "Flag Birthday" on June 14, the anniversary of the adoption of the flag design that we know as the Stars and Stripes. Following the lead of teachers and other advocates, Flag Day on June 14 grew in popularity as well as official stature.

By the late nineteenth century, state governments in New York, Pennsylvania, and Illinois were marking June 14 as Flag Day, with many ceremonies centering on schoolchildren who would gather to sing patriotic songs, march, or wear small flags. According to the website usflag.org, "On June 14, 1894, . . . the first general public school children's celebration of Flag Day in Chicago was held in Douglas, Garfield, Humboldt, Lincoln, and Washington Parks, with more than 300,000 children participating. Adults, too, participated in patriotic programs. Franklin K. Lane, Secretary of the Interior, delivered a 1914 Flag Day address in which he repeated words he said the flag had spoken to him that morning: 'I am what you make me; nothing more. I swing before your eyes as a bright gleam of color, a symbol of yourself.'"

In 1916, President Woodrow Wilson issued a proclamation establishing Flag Day nationally on June 14. Finally, decades later, Congress enacted legislation that officially designated June 14 as the national Flag Day, and the measure was signed into law by President Harry Truman in 1949. The act also called upon the president to issue a Flag Day proclamation every year. Although we do not get a day off from work, Flag Day continues to be marked by schools, municipalities, civic organizations, and patriotic Americans throughout the land.

Another such occasion is the annual Juneteenth celebration observed by many African Americans and their fellow Americans. Juneteenth, celebrated on June 19, commemorates the ending of slavery in the United States. The observance began in 1865, in Galveston, Texas. The particular date of June 19 was chosen because it was the day the Union soldiers, under Major General Gordon Granger, landed at Galveston with news that the war had ended and that the enslaved were now free. Over the years, Juneteenth celebrations have waxed and waned, with a notable resurgence in recent years focusing on the spiritual and family aspects of the holiday.

The Catholic Church also celebrates some important feast days during the summer months. Two Apostles, who were so instrumental in laying the foundation of the Church, have been honored together going as far back as the third or fourth century. June 29 is used because it notes the date that the remains of Saints Peter and Paul were transferred to particular catacombs in Rome, a common practice in determining when to honor a particular saint on the Church's liturgical calendar.

Pope Benedict XVI proclaimed a Jubilee Year of St. Paul, from June 28, 2008, to June 29, 2009, to mark the two-thousandth anniversary of Paul's birth. Churches in the United States and throughout the world honored the occasion, especially churches whose patrons are Saints Peter and Paul. In England and Wales, the Feast of Saints Peter and Paul is a holy day of obligation.

If Memorial Day is the unofficial start to summer in the United States, then the July 4 celebration is when summer begins in earnest. School is out. Vacations are scheduled. *Homo ludens* is in charge. Leisure reigns. The national celebrations take on a quasi-religious aspect.

July 4, or Independence Day, underscores the importance of marking a special day as an unmovable feast, if you will. If we as Christians recognize confusion about exactly when Christ was born, we can understand a similar confusion applying to the birth of our own nation. We celebrate July 4 as the birthday of the United States of America because that is the day when the Second Continental Congress voted its approval of the Declaration of Independence at the Pennsylvania State House (now Independence Hall) in Philadelphia.

Notably, the Declaration of Independence was not signed until August 2 (and even then not by all who would eventually sign the document). One could suggest August 2, then, as a valid date for celebrating independence. Going further, one might argue that such dates were pointless until the Revolutionary War was over. Following that line of reasoning, perhaps we should celebrate our national birthday on September 3, when the Treaty of Paris was signed in 1783. Going further yet, the United States did not become a nation as we know it today until the Constitution of the United States was adopted by all the states.

Why, then, don't we celebrate our nation's birthday on September 17, the date the U.S. Constitution was signed, or December 15, the date that three-fourths of the states had ratified the Bill of Rights? And so on. The fact is, both traditions and laws, myths and realities, come into play not only in determining religious feasts but in determining secular ones as well. Once the Declaration of Independence was read aloud throughout the Colonies, and once the War of Independence was won, tradition took hold. (Plus, the printed copy of the draft approved on July 4 starts off with "In Congress, July 4, 1776 . . .") The Fourth of July was the day to celebrate our independence, focusing on the document that expressed the spiritual as well as political foundation of the new nation.

Celebrations of American independence have varied widely both in the United States and even in other countries around the world. Curiously, it was not a national holiday until 1941. So, as with Christmas, factual information is far from the only reason that people settle upon a fixed date for marking a feast. Celebrations, which echo traditional Christian practices (hot dog-eating aside), have included the following notable events:

- The Independence Day parade in Bristol, Rhode Island, is the longest such continuous celebration in the United States, having begun in 1785.
- Since 1843, Lititz, Pennsylvania, holds elaborate festivities around Independence Day featuring a Queen of Candles who presides over thousands of floating candles on water.
- For three days over the Fourth, Native Americans gather in Flagstaff, Arizona, a tradition that goes back to the 1880s.
- In Coney Island, New York, Nathan's has sponsored an annual Fourth of July hot dog-eating contest.
- Since 1912, a Danish-American friendship group has marked the feast in Copenhagen.

If the summer holidays pay homage to *homo ludens,* then the end of summer tips its hat to *homo faber,* working man. Labor Day, which is marked on the first Monday in September, owes its origins to a movement in Canada. In the United States, its chief advocate was Peter J. McGuire of New York City, the president of the United Brotherhood of Carpenters and Joiners of America labor union. His suggestion in 1882 was to observe "a festive day during which a parade through the streets of the city would permit public tribute to American industry."

The September date was selected for reasons of anticipated good weather and to differentiate it from May 1, its European counterpart. In 1882, New York held such a parade, and the idea spread to other cities; soon states such as Oregon, Colorado, Massachusetts, New York, and New Jersey proclaimed state holidays. By 1928, all the states except Wyoming embraced the idea. Today it is a federal and state holiday.

Labor Day came about not without controversy, however. The late nineteenth century endured many clashes of workers and company owners, often marked by many deaths, as workers fought for paid holidays, vacations, eight-hour work days, and basic protections for health and safety. Therefore, Labor Day held symbolic importance for the common person, for those who worked in factories and fields making America's goods and products.

This national holiday, then, has come to symbolize the end of summer, the end of the time for *homo ludens*. It's back to work, back to school, back to *homo faber*.

But for a spirited, exuberant, and pranksterish minority, *homo ludens* has the last word. For the week before and including Labor Day weekend, every year tens of thousands of participants—there were more than 48,000 in 2009—gather for an event called Burning Man in the Black Rock Desert, about 120 miles north of Reno, Nevada. It has no rules, except for those about health and safety. Although admission tickets are sold, it is not about selling things (only coffee and ice are sold there). It is, rather, more about anarchic and creative expression, artistry, destruction, survival, and wildness.

Burning Man is radical yet collective individualism. It is said that there are no spectators allowed. The radical event gets its name from the deliberate burning of a 40-foot statue of a neon-festooned man on the Saturday before Labor Day. The event started at Baker Beach in San Francisco in 1986 and moved to the Nevada desert in the early 1990s. After the event, the participants dismantle and leave the temporary city, leaving as few traces as possible in the Nevada desert.

As extreme and limit-pushing as the event is, Burning Man has elements that resemble liturgy, that follow codes and guidelines for the common good. In short, although pagan in many aspects, Burning Man underscores our deep desire for expression, freedom, individuality, creativity, and play. It sees play as holy, if you will. And in that sense, one could argue that certain aspects of Burning Man, however far they are from traditional religion, echo many of the tribal traits of religion. It shows how much we yearn to be *homo ludens* in today's *homo faber* world.

SUMMER SAINTS

As in every month or season of the year, the summer months of Ordinary Time contain plenty of inspiring and unique feasts and saints' memorials:

July 4 is also the memorial of St. John Mary Vianney, the parish priest, or *cure*, of Ars, France, who is revered as the patron of priests and pastors.

Blessed Kateri Tekakwitha, virgin (July 14), was born in 1656, the daughter of a Mohawk warrior in what is now upstate New York. She died in 1680, four years after she had been baptized a Catholic. She lived in a Christian colony in Canada and dedicated her life to prayer and care for the sick and was also known as "Lily of the Mohawks." She was beatified in 1980, the penultimate stage before formal canonization by the Church.

St. Mary Magdalene, disciple of Christ (July 22), is one of the most fascinating and controversial saints in the canon, thanks in large degree to the notoriety of Dan Brown's international bestseller, *The Da Vinci Code*. In the novel, the Catholic Church has purportedly engaged in a centuries-old cover-up of the marriage between Mary Magdalene and Jesus—and the birth of a daughter from that union who is the "Holy Grail," or the "royal bloodline." Pope Gregory I is reviled by some modern exegetes for consigning Mary Magdalene to the status of a prostitute. She is honored by many as an Apostle and perhaps was closest to Christ.

Joachim and Anne are the names given by ancient tradition to the parents of the Virgin Mary (July 26). St. Anne is the only woman in history, other than Mary herself, to give birth to a child born without Original Sin. She is honored by some Italian-American communities with a midsummer festival.

For Catholics, two Marian feasts occur before Labor Day. The Solemnity of the Assumption of the Virgin Mary into Heaven is August 15, a celebration by the Church of the doctrine that Mary did not die but was taken bodily into heaven. Pope Pius XII declared this dogma (infallibly, according to the First Vatican Council) in 1950. The Blessed Virgin is patron of Guatemala, Panama, and Paraguay under this title of the Assumption.

Then, on August 22, as students begin to return to the classroom, comes the Memorial of the Queenship of the Virgin Mary, the octave of the Assumption. Do you see a pattern here? Once she was assumed into heaven she took up her place as queen, one of the most revered and powerful models, intercessors, and patrons for believers on earth.

Three more major Marian feasts are clustered in September. The Feast of the Birth of Mary is September 8. We cannot know when she was born, but we know that she was! Now an optional feast, the Most Holy Name of the Blessed Virgin Mary is marked on September 12. Beginning in 1863, it honored the name of the baby girl born four days earlier, then it was suppressed (dropped from the liturgical calendar), then restored as an optional observance by Pope

John Paul II. The Memorial of Our Lady of Sorrows is celebrated on September 15, invoking the image of Mary at the
foot of the cross, recalling the prophecy that a sword of sorrow shall pierce her heart.

THE "LORD'S DAY"
AND KEEPING IT HOLY

A bishop's function in the Roman Catholic Church is to maintain the integrity of the *magisterium*, which is the teaching authority of the Church, and to bring the Eucharist to the people through his representatives, the parish priests. In the course of his duties, the bishop is called upon to preach to the people and to write pastoral letters as their chief pastor.

On March 17, 2010, Archbishop Timothy M. Dolan of New York published such a letter. The immediate occasion was the celebration of St. Patrick's Day—an important festival in New York City, where so many Irish-Americans flourish—but the main topic was the Sabbath. He said that "to look at how we are living the Catholic faith that has been handed on to us by so many generations . . . might I suggest that we look together at one important aspect of living our Catholic faith, namely the *Lord's Day*?" This, of course, means Sunday.

I have previously discussed the importance of Sundays in the liturgical calendar of the Church—how Sunday has traditionally been set aside as a day of required attendance at Mass and a cessation of work. It is a day of rest, mirroring God's own example on the seventh day of his creation of the world in which we live.

Archbishop Dolan has presented his flock with an in-depth reflection that can profitably serve as the basis for our present purposes of exploring the Catholic origin and meanings of holidays and holy days. He writes:

> *Anybody 50 or older can remember when faithful attendance at Sunday Mass was the norm for all Catholics. To miss Sunday Eucharist, unless you were sick, was unheard of. To be a "practicing Catholic" meant you were at Mass every Sunday. Over 75% of Catholics went to Mass every Sunday.*
>
> *That should still be the case. Sadly, it is not. Now, the studies tell us, only one-third of us go weekly, perhaps even less in some areas of the archdiocese [of New York].*
>
> *If you want your faith to wither up and die quit going to Sunday Mass. As the body will die without food, the soul will expire without nourishment. That sustenance comes at the Sunday Eucharist.*

Archbishop Dolan summarizes the position of the Church—and its contemporary lament—here. National studies show that only one-fourth to one-third of Catholics attend Mass each Sunday, despite the fact that it is required by their faith that they do so. Why? Well, in the first decade of the twenty-first century, many point to how the ugly sex-abuse scandals disturbed the faithful and kept many away—a problem that, unfortunately, continues today. Rules are now relaxed everywhere, at home, on the job, and in society at large, affecting those with a more lackadaisical attitude toward their faith. Not to mention that the quality of faith, of teaching, of urgency has diminished in some churches and in some individuals. There is also no sense that meaningful sanctions apply against those who do not attend. And sometimes recreation or work take priority over Mass.

Nonetheless, Catholics remain under obligation to attend Mass on Sundays and other non-Sunday holy days observed by this requirement, including the solemnities of the Immaculate Conception, the Nativity of the Lord (Christmas), and Mary, the Mother of God.

THE SABBATH: ROOTS IN JUDAISM

Since the historic Second Vatican Council, held in St. Peter's Basilica in Rome between 1962 and 1965, the Church has explicitly condemned anti-Semitism in all forms and encouraged dialogue and respect among Jews and Christians.

This was a necessary antidote to the poison of centuries and the unspeakable destruction of the Jewish population of Europe in the Holocaust. For too long, too many Christians had, at best, turned a blind eye to overt prejudice against Jews and at worst, actively participated in their persecution. *Nostra Aetate,* the Declaration on the Relation of the Church to Non-Christian Religions, was issued by the Council in 1965. Immediately the Church's relationship with Jews and Judaism entered a new phase.

Catholics are taught to recognize Jews as "elder brothers in the faith," as a people who remain chosen of God, whose covenant, while "old," remains in effect. The Jewish people are a gift from God and give many gifts to the world. One is the traditional observance of the Sabbath, which "is now, and has been since time immemorial, a constitutive part of being a Jew. Even if many Jews today, like Catholics, no longer observe the Sabbath, it remains a distinctive mark of identity," according to Rabbi Abraham Joshua Heschel in his book *The Sabbath.*

There are few ideas in the history of the world that contain as much spiritual power as the notion of the Sabbath. The Sabbath provides the sought-after link between the created and the Creator, with each acknowledging the other. We, on the human side of the equation, express our gratitude through worship and observance of rites that take us out of our normal routine and focus our minds—our entire beings—on things spiritual.

We are more than our work. As Rabbi Heschel teaches: "The Sabbath is a day for the sake of life. Man is not a beast of burden, and the Sabbath is not for the purpose of enhancing the efficiency of his work . . . the Sabbath is not for the sake of the weekdays; the weekdays are for the sake of the Sabbath. It is not an interlude, but the climax of living."

THE WEEKEND

The weekend and five-day work week, to which we have become accustomed over the course of the past century and more, have their roots in this theology and practice—but with distinctly secular and even political implications.

In his own apostolic letter *Dies Domini* (the Lord's Day), promulgated in 1998, Pope John Paul II wrote:

> *The custom of the "weekend" has become more widespread, a weekly period of respite, spent perhaps far from home and often involving participation in cultural, political or sporting activities, which are usually held on free days. This social and cultural phenomenon is by no means without its positive aspects if, while respecting true values, it can contribute to people's development and to the advancement of the life of society as a whole. All of this responds not only to the need for rest, but also to the need for celebration, which is inherent in our humanity.*
>
> *Unfortunately, when Sunday loses its fundamental meaning and becomes merely part of a "weekend," it can happen that*

people stay locked within a horizon so limited that they can no longer see the heavens. Hence, though ready to celebrate, they are really incapable of doing so. The disciples of Christ, however, are asked to avoid any confusion between the celebration of Sunday, which should truly be a way of keeping the Lord's Day holy, and the "weekend," understood as a time of simple rest and relaxation.

Can you see the emphasis that Pope John Paul II, Archbishop Timothy Dolan, and Rabbi Abraham Joshua Heschel all offer? They call persons of faith to reorient themselves nearly 180 degrees to consider the Sabbath, whether that is the seventh day or the first day of the week, as the fulcrum of existence rather than an afterthought.

THE CHURCH AND SUNDAY

"Just as the Sabbath—the seventh day of God's rest—united the Jewish people and marked the covenant, Sunday expresses what most of us believe as disciples of Jesus Christ. We proclaim the Risen Christ, and so our time is marked by Sunday, the first day of the week, the first day of a new creation, the day of a new covenant," Archbishop Dolan wrote in his pastoral letter.

Do Catholics live for Sunday? he asks. Is it the "climax" of our lives?

This is why the Church spends so much time urging Catholics to be in church on Sunday. In fact, the Church (as an institution and as a collection of fallible human beings) cannot understand why its members are not clamoring to fill the pews.

Well, we have listed some of the reasons American Catholics are disaffected these days, and they are not insignificant or to be dismissed lightly. Yet, as always with matters of faith, the obligation to seek, to ask, to act, to *move* in the right direction falls on the individual believer. At the Sunday liturgy, all the members of the Church stand together to proclaim what they believe.

Further, for the past century, the popes have encouraged frequent reception of Holy Communion (the Eucharist) by Catholics—which means at least once per week, on Sunday. The rules of fasting and preparation for reception have been relaxed to make it easier for everyone to receive the sacrament. The flip side of this coin is that some approach the altar to take the host—and the cup—with a less than reverent attitude.

"THREATS" TO SUNDAY

Archbishop Dolan acknowledges that today there are many threats to Sunday observance. The more obvious ones may be easier to tackle head on. Do people really need to work on Sunday? For some there may be little or no choice in the matter. The responsibility to earn a livelihood to support one's family takes precedence over nearly everything else.

But other obvious challenges to keeping the day holy are recreational commitments, in particular children's sports and other activities. "At the very least," the archbishop argues, "children's activities should be organized in a way that permits the family to go to Mass together, if possible. There is no denying that this will occasion some sacrifice, but the development of a child is not well-served by indicating that Sunday Mass is secondary to other things."

From Sunday, then, as the first day of the week, the meaning of the balance of the week is derived. The coming together of the faithful "sets up" the pattern for the rest of the days: to include prayer during the day, whether the Catholic attends formal services (daily Mass) or participates in the Liturgy of the Hours in some form of community, or even alone.

Sunday is supposed to be unlike any other day, to be anticipated and celebrated in a unique way. It is a holy day and a holiday in the fullest sense of each. The idea of obligation is, in the eyes of the Church, very real—but it should be taken not as an oppressive legalism to make Sunday a day of dread but as a day of joy. The obligation should be viewed by the faithful as a constant opportunity for spiritual growth, as well as recreation.

Laurence Hull Stookey offers a "modest if unusual proposal" to solve the dilemma of Sunday:

Suppose that mentally we shift the way we calculate time, at least on the weekends, and recover our Hebraic heritage of reckoning days from sunset to sunset. Mentally ending the Lord's Day at sunset on Sunday allows for the necessary Sunday evening tasks to be done as a part of the work of the second day of the Christian week. But more important, to discipline ourselves to regard the Lord's Day as beginning on Saturday evening allows time for spiritual preparation that cannot be squeezed into the schedules of most church-going families the next morning. Such a reordering of Christian thinking, contrary as it is to prevailing cultural customs, could be the beginning of a new way of seeing the whole of Christian faith as a reinterpretation of commonly accepted ideas and values.

Yes, the Christian observance of Sunday has become "countercultural" in our time. Bishops and rabbis seek to reclaim the Judeo-Christian claim on the soul of the believer for one day per week. What is our response to be?

[Extended excerpts from Archbishop Dolan's letter of March 27, 2010, are reprinted here with permission of the Archdiocese of New York.]

PART IV

FALL

Autumn harvests and the inexorable shortening of days herald yet another change in the eternal cycle of the seasons. The days the Church calls Ordinary Time continue until the end of the liturgical year on Christ the King Sunday.

Of course, Halloween is a wonderful, climactic holiday, especially for kids who get the chance to dress up in costumes and assume new identities, if only for one night, and, with more than a hint of mischief in the air, go trick-or-treating. For them—and perhaps for most adults—the theology of the evening and its origin haven't really entered their minds.

That's okay. Harkening back to harvest festivals in ancient times and the Middle Ages, the public marking of the days assumed a religious underpinning and was administered by priests (in Celtic lands, the Druidic class) as a matter of custom.

For Christians in poor countries or regions, or during difficult times of drought or plague, the local church was a refuge, a place of prayer and hope, and a collection point for charity, if such was available at all. There was nowhere else to go.

In our time, autumn also brings a retrenchment, a return to school, and a hunkering-down before the onset of winter. It is a time of intense recreation, at least in the Northern Hemisphere, again echoing customs and survival techniques of earlier ages dependent upon hunting and agriculture. In the United States, football on all levels, from Pop Warner League to National Football League, takes on a near-religious aura during crisp afternoons and evenings on Friday, Saturday, and Sunday.

Fall is also a season of dying and falling leaves, harvest and storage of supplies for the dark, cold times to come. Church and society mark it as such, with a bit more solemnity than at other times of the year, as the days grow shorter and the trees barer with each passing sunset.

CHAPTER 12

HALLOWEEN

Before we don our masks to go trick-or-treating, let's pause at the word—and the idea of—"Halloween." The word itself encapsulates the story of this holy day or holiday.

As early as 1389 we find an instance of the word "Hallowmas," a reference to All Saints' Day, "hallow" being an archaic word for holy, as in "hallowed be thy name" from the Lord's Prayer. Over the years we find an evolution in print, seeing terms such as "Allhallow-even," meaning the evening before All Saints' Day.

By 1745, we encounter the shorter Scottish form of the word, "Hallowe'en," with the apostrophe standing in for the *v* in "even." In 1785, the poet Robert Burns even published a poem titled "Halloween." The *Oxford English Dictionary* cites in its definition an 1883 article in *Harper's* magazine that declares, "Halloween is the carnival-time of disembodied spirits."

Just as many Catholics choose to celebrate the Sunday Eucharist on the vigil, or evening, before, so may we view the celebration of Halloween. From the perspective of the Church it is simply the vigil of a major feast, All Saints' Day.

Alas, the story does not end there; it is just the beginning.

What is it, then—pagan feast, Catholic holy day, or secular holiday?

Despite its unmistakable attachment to the Catholic liturgical commemoration of All Saints' Day, Halloween is also a word with ancient, spooky, and pagan connotations. That is because its history, perhaps more than most holidays and holy days, has one foot in the sacred and another in the profane. But it is a bit more complex than that.

Many Christians complain about Halloween's "pagan origins," with some going so far as to oppose Halloween celebrations. But as noted elsewhere in this book, no one is surprised at this. Christianity has a rich history of co-opting pagan or pre-Christian holidays and transforming them for the Church's own purposes (even the Hebrews of old did the same). This is partly owing to cultural and political reasons as well as religious ones. Of course, its co-opting of holidays symbolizes the ascendancy of the early Church as it sought to establish its dominance over secular or pagan influences—in the same way that the Christmas tree came to symbolize Christian truths instead of pagan rituals.

Halloween clearly coincides with, and overtakes, an ancient Celtic holy day. The feast of Samhain (pronounced *SOW-win*) was a new year's feast for the ancient Druids of the western British Isles. This region comprises present-day Ireland, Wales, the highlands of Scotland, and Brittany in northwest France.

Samhain marked the end of summer and the beginning of winter. November 1 was the beginning of the new year. Samhain was the Druids' Lord of the Dead, whose feast was celebrated on November 1. On that day tribute was also paid to the sun god of the Celts.

Incidentally, even in contemporary Gaelic, the month of November is referred to by the word "Samhain." The Samhain festival has also been associated with Maeve, the Irish heroine of epic myths and the goddess of beginnings.

Samhain had its own rites, liturgies, games—as any feast of ancient peoples would. Horses were sacrificed to the sun god. Fire burned on special mounds. Food was left for wandering spirits from the other world beyond the grave. According to the Venerable Bede's *Ecclesiastical History of the English People,* Pope Gregory the Great in the sixth century instructed the faithful in Britain that "the sacrifice of oxen in pagan worship should be allowed to continue, but that this should be done in honor of the saints and sacred relics."

It is likely, therefore, that this practice continued at least for a while.

In the next few centuries the conjoining of Samhain with All Saints' Day began to take shape as the Church asserted its dominance. In 731 Pope Gregory III dedicated an oratory to all the saints in Saint Peter's in Rome, declaring that every year on November 1 a Mass celebrating all the saints should be held. In the ninth century Pope Gregory IV put the feast on the Church's calendar, and his successor, Pope Sixtus IV, made All Saints' Day a holy day of obligation.

But Halloween and All Saints' Day have long shared a connection with All Souls' Day, November 2, when the Church remembers the dead. This association further mingles with the Samhain practices that engaged spirits from the other world. Tradition holds that St. Odilon, abbot of Cluny, was a key figure in establishing All Souls' Day in 998, which Pope John Paul II commemorated in a special way on November 2, 1998, a thousand years later.

The links between Halloween and All Saints' and All Souls' Days allow us to reflect on the concept of purgatory. For the pre-Christian Celts, there was no hell or heaven. Death was considered as only the middle of a long life. Everyone was entitled to make the passage to the other world we call death. It wasn't considered a matter of judgment or punishment.

Many scholars agree that the Irish influence on the Church brought us the notion of purgatory. In the fifth century, St. Patrick wrote of a vision of the other world and the monks of St. Columba added to a tradition that has echoes of the spirits we see roaming on the eve of Samhain. From the Druids' perspective, the spirits who roam on Halloween/Samhain are suffering because they have not completed their role or finished their journey. They are asking for help from us, the living, to finish their journey to the other world.

Keep in mind that the pre-Christian Celts believed in three natural elements: water, earth, and air. In fact one scholar makes a connection of purgatory to the Greek word for fire, reminding us of the Samhain sacred fires that marked the beginning of the dark season. Therefore, it is only natural that on the night of October 31 and the days of November 1 and November 2, the Church and its pagan heritage would coexist, albeit uncomfortably at times.

As historian Jean Markale puts it:

> The world of the dead was open to the living and vice versa; time was abolished; and ghosts, a convenient term for spiritual entities seeking contact with humans, could temporarily materialize and engage in dialogue.

This is not unlike the Christian practice of praying for the souls in purgatory. In the afterlife, some souls who are destined for heaven but not quite "ready" are sent to purgatory in order to be fully cleansed of sin.

It [the holiday] is a way of . . . exorcising [death] by establishing a direct line between before and after, which will display the permanence of life in all its aspects and all its states. This is the appropriate lesson to draw from Samhain and its survivals, whether the Christian All Saints' Day or the folklore manifestations of Halloween.

Because they observed Samhain, we can thank the Irish for many of the ways that Americans celebrate Halloween. Halloween as we know it in this country began to be celebrated after the wave of Irish immigrants streamed here on account of the potato famine of the 1840s. Again, many of the traditions bear the marks of Celtic heritage as expressed at Samhain, as well as the full embrace of Catholic values.

One tradition, of course, involves the masks and costumes worn by children. According to some, masks were worn around Halloween to imitate the saints. Wealthy parishes, such as in Wittenberg, Germany, had the relics of many saints that they could display at All Saints' Day. But poorer churches did not have enough money to pay for saints' relics, so they held processions with parishioners who dressed up as their patronal saints, as well as portraying angels or devils as everyone paraded around the churchyard.

Similarly, on the eve of All Souls' Day (in other words, All Saints' night), children were known to travel around wearing masks as they offered to fast for the good of souls in purgatory, for which they would often receive money or offerings. Along these lines, "trick or treat" rituals from the Middle Ages did much the same, with "soul cakes" being offered to please the dead in order that they would do no mischief, or tricks.

The tradition of the jack-o'-lantern is another that reflects a mix of pagan and Christian perspectives. It comes to us from an Irish folktale. Briefly, it is the story of a reprobate known as Jack, who was known to make bargains with the devil. As a result of his selfish misdeeds, Jack was consigned to wander the earth—trapped eternally between heaven and hell. This was because heaven rejected him for his drunken ways and stinginess; he stayed out of hell because the devil owed him a favor from an earlier bargain.

One Irish legend has it that upon Jack's return from hell, the devil tossed him a live coal, as a remembrance. He was eating a turnip and placed the coal inside it. In America, the hollowed-out turnip became a pumpkin, and Jack wanders the earth looking for a place to rest. Naturally, it is not hard to see how Christians would derive lessons from this tale, ranging from the new fire of the Easter Vigil to praying for the souls in purgatory. And of course the candles seen in today's Halloween pumpkins easily serve to remind us that the candle is also a Christian symbol.

The Mexican celebration of the Day of the Dead, or Día de los Muertos is very different from the Irish take on the holiday. Although not strictly a Halloween celebration, this feast spans All Saints' and All Souls' Day with touches of our traditional Halloween. In this culture, the event is festive, with lots of food and joyful visits to dead relatives at cemeteries. As with the Irish and European contributions to Halloween, many people don colorful costumes.

In both cases, the ancient secular traditions are intertwined with the eve of All Saints' on the Church calendar.

American culture continues to put great emphasis on Halloween; the holiday ranks second only to Christmas in terms of its economic impact. Hollywood has catered to this (*Halloween I, Halloween II,* etc.), with a twist shown by Tim Burton's *The Nightmare Before Christmas,* a movie with a dark side but with many themes of death and rebirth and a basic understanding that Halloween and Christmas are both new year's feasts at heart.

One of the most memorable takes on the day is the 1966 television special *It's the Great Pumpkin, Charlie Brown,* based on the popular Charles Schulz comic strip, "Peanuts." In the animated film, Charlie's friend Linus believes that the "Great Pumpkin" will appear on Halloween, bringing gifts, as Santa Claus does on Christmas Eve. But when Linus doubts for a brief second, the Pumpkin does not appear. Linus tells Charlie that certainly the Great Pumpkin will come—*next* year . . .

Halloween has been at the center of many so-called culture wars of recent decades. The viewpoints vary widely. *Witch City,* a film documentary of the early 1990s, shows a Christian anti-Halloween parade featuring a flatbed truck with a crucified Jesus bearing the inscription, "This blood's for you." On the one hand, Salem, Massachusetts, site of the notorious witchcraft trials and executions of the seventeenth century, shamelessly promotes itself as a Halloween capital, while Los Altos, California banned teaching about Halloween in 1995, then reversed itself, ultimately deciding that Halloween was not a religious holiday (an irony that also arises in discussions of Christmas displays in the public square).

Some local churches, in Colorado for example, have set up so-called hell houses at Halloween to graphically oppose abortion or make other statements, but the Colorado Council of Churches weighed in, saying that such displays went too far.

Although many Christian groups decry Halloween's pagan origins, some see opportunities for teaching. A Catholic website, www.americancatholic.org notes, "There's no reason to fear skeletons, skulls or Thomas More with his head tucked under his arm. After all, can't skulls and skeletons be healthy reminders of human mortality? Can't witches and devils symbolize the evil Christ has overcome?"

Some anti-Halloween disciples have used the attacks as opportunities for frankly anti-Catholic diatribes. Evangelist Jack T. Chick and others have published tracts on the "history" of Halloween, alleging Halloween satanic sacrifices and mixing in falsehoods about Catholic beliefs and practices.

This religious hostility has some cultural roots in that the "rational" English, including the early Colonial Puritans, have long been suspicious of the Irish, Celtic, and Druidic and their more mystical, less "rational" rituals.

The Roman Catholic Church officially says little about Halloween. Any direct statements by popes are nonexistent. However, the Church's uneasy alliance with this feast continues. In 1999, French bishops issued a statement condemning the carnival-like celebrations of Halloween.

However, the Vatican's official daily newspaper, *L'Osservatore Romano*, made a stir in 2009 when it quoted a Spanish cleric, Father Joan Maria Canals, with a story headlined "Halloween's Dangerous Messages." The story quotes Father Canals: "Halloween has an undercurrent of occultism and is absolutely anti-Christian."

Parents were advised not to allow their kids to dress up as ghosts or goblins and told to turn away from "terror, fear and death." And in the preceding year, a newspaper reportedly controlled by Italy's bishops urged a boycott of Halloween, calling it a "dangerous celebration of horror and the macabre," and warning that Halloween could encourage "pitiless [satanic] sects without scruples."

And yet where some see doom, others see opportunity. In 1999, Sister Maureen Shaughnessy, assistant secretary for catechesis and leadership formation for the U.S. Bishops' department of education, issued a statement: "Halloween gives us the opportunity to help people of all ages reconnect with the Christian understanding of this very popular holiday. Originally this day was celebrated by the Celts in England

and Ireland as the end of their year. On that day they remembered all those who had died during the past year."

The U.S. Bishops' office of media relations at the time went on to say, "A number of customs that evolved related to this had to do with ghosts and scary things. As Christians we celebrate this day as the eve of All Saints, and in fact, many parishes and Catholic schools use this opportunity to have young people connect to the lives of saints—their own name saints or patronal saints connected to their parishes or ethnic backgrounds. It provides a time for storytelling, dressing up and celebrating."

From this perspective, Halloween is seen as a chance to reinforce Catholic values in a secular world.

Perhaps Halloween more than any other holiday illustrates that we are products of our culture, for good or ill. Our culture influences our religious practices, and vice versa. This has been true from the beginnings of Christianity—and even for the Israelites in biblical times. A striking example of this was exhibited by Americans in 2001. After the terrorist attacks in New York, Washington, D.C., and Pennsylvania, Americans marked Halloween in a distinctly subdued manner. We saw jack-o'-lanterns with stars and stripes; we saw Osama bin Laden demonized on masks; we remembered dead victims and heroes of the attacks.

For many, Halloween was again truly All Hallows Eve.

CHAPTER 13

ANGELS AND SAINTS

Catholics believe that angels are heavenly messengers, defenders, and helpers sent by God to men and women on earth. The Catechism of the Catholic Church states explicitly: "The existence of the spiritual, non-corporeal beings that Sacred Scripture usually calls 'angels' is a truth of faith. The witness of Scripture is as clear as the unanimity of Tradition."

St. Augustine of Hippo writes, "'Angel' is the name of their office, not of their nature. If you seek the name of their nature, it is 'spirit'; if you seek the name of their office, it is 'angel'; from what they are, 'spirit,' from what they do, 'angel.'"

Angels most often figure in Bible narratives as servants and messengers, and they are said to be attendants at the throne of God. But we receive few glimpses of them throughout the Old and New Testaments. In the latter, angels are present at the birth of Jesus as a heavenly chorus singing, *"Gloria in excelsis Deo!"* And some nine months previously, the Archangel Gabriel appeared to the young virgin Mary to announce that she would bear the Son of God.

The archangels, of whom there are three named in the Bible (with the distinctive "-el" at the end of the name), are the highest ranking and most powerful of all the angels. Among them, St. Michael is the leader, a sort of "general"— and the patron saint of police officers. His leadership stemmed from the time of Lucifer's fall from grace, and Michael is often portrayed as driving the evil angel from heaven into the fire of hell. The other two major archangels are Gabriel, the messenger to Mary, and Raphael, who specialized in expelling demons from those possessed.

September 29 is the Feast of Saints Michael, Gabriel, and Raphael. The feast originally was Michael's alone, and the readings for the Mass of the day refer exclusively to him, since the feast derived from the day on which the Roman basilica named for Michael was dedicated.

War broke out in heaven;
Michael and his angels battled against the dragon.
The dragon and its angels fought back,
but they did not prevail
and there was no longer any place for them in heaven.
The huge dragon, the ancient serpent,
who is called the Devil and Satan,

who deceived the whole world,

was thrown down to earth,

and the angels were thrown down with it.

—*Revelation 12:7–9*

According to the old *Catholic Encyclopedia*, the Feast of Guardian Angels, October 4, "like many others, was local before it was placed in the Roman calendar. But . . . among the earliest petitions from particular churches to be allowed, as a supplement to [the] breviary, the canonical celebration of local feasts, was a request from Cordova in 1579 for permission to have a feast in honor of the guardian angels."

Pope Paul V inserted this feast into the canon (that is, the official list) on the first available day after the Feast of St. Michael the Archangel. Then, among numerous changes made to the calendar by Clement X was the elevation of the Feast of Guardian Angels to the rank of an obligatory observance for the whole Church, to be kept on October 2. Finally, Pope Leo XIII raised the feast to the rank of a "double [or duplex] major" in 1883 (a double major has to do with having two antiphons in the Liturgy of the Hours, or the breviary).

Of guardian angels, we read in the Catechism of the Catholic Church: "From infancy to death human life is surrounded by their watchful care and intercession. 'Beside each believer stands an angel as protector and shepherd leading him to life.'" That latter quote within the quote is from the writings of St. Basil, an early Church Father. An important daily devotion involving angels is the thrice-daily prayer called the Angelus, which recounts, in a longer form than the short Hail Mary prayer, the appearance of the angel to the Blessed Virgin. It divides the waking day into thirds, and was useful in a very public way during the Middle Ages. It remains in many people's memories as the moment on the Catholic school playground when all activity stopped, with the tolling of the church's bells at noon; that, too, was a public moment, with a few hundred kids genuflecting in prayer in the parking-lot playground.

Angels play a part in popular culture, including in television programs such as *Touched by an Angel, Highway to Heaven,* and *Saving Grace.* Each features an appealing and unusual character, an angel who plays the role of guardian and protector to the protagonist. In the 1990s and early 2000s, numerous books, some serious, some lighthearted, touched on the subject, and somber films such as *Legion* (2010) brought angels to life on the big screen.

Are angels among us? Look around. You might see one in your life . . .

The Roman Catholic Church venerates saints as those who have followed the words of Jesus Christ and been faithful members of his body. The Church is, indeed, in its own words the "body of Christ" and the "communion of saints." We have seen throughout the year how saints' days are observed in their own right, as they have been for many centuries, or transmuted into secular holidays after further centuries of custom and tradition. In Fred Pratt Green's hymn "The Saints: Who Are They? And Why Are They?" he writes:

Rejoice in God's saints, today and all days
a world without saints forgets how to praise.

According to St. Paul in the New Testament, any believer is called a "saint," one who has been sanctified with the grace of God, touched by the Holy Spirit, infused with faith. Paul calls the followers of Christ in Corinth "saints."

Again, the Catechism of the Catholic Church comes to our rescue with this explanation: "When the Church keeps the memorials of martyrs and other saints during the annual cycle, she proclaims the Paschal mystery in those who have suffered and have been glorified with Christ. She proposes them to the faithful as examples who draw all men to the Father through Christ, and through their merits she begs for God's favors."

Most often, saints' days are chosen to coincide with the death date, or the day that saint entered into his or her new and eternal life.

Chief in precedence among the saints are the Apostles—because they were the first witnesses to the person and ministry of Jesus. (St. Paul is the exception, though he claimed a vision of the risen Lord at his conversion.) St. Matthias was chosen by lot to take the place of the Apostle Judas, who betrayed Christ.

Therefore, from the earliest days, the Church that they founded (or, perhaps more aptly, the *churches* they founded in numerous cities throughout the Mediterranean region and western Asia) remembered and revered them and created the means to carry forward their reputations with festivals, or "feast days."

The Apostles' days unfold throughout the year as follows:

January 25	Conversion of Paul
February 22	Chair of Peter
May 3	Philip and James the Lesser (son of Alphaeus)
May 14	Matthias
June 11	Barnabas
June 29	Peter and Paul
July 3	Thomas
July 25	James the Greater (son of Zebedee)
August 24	Bartholomew
September 21	Matthew
October 28	Simon and Jude (also called Thaddeus)
November 30	Andrew
December 27	John

In addition to these preeminent figures—and a few others, such as Mary Magdalene—the martyrs, beginning with St. Stephen (whose memorial is December 26), are perhaps the most revered saints: those who gave their lives for the sake of their faith in Jesus. And that is really just the tip of the iceberg.

To the faithful of antiquity and the Middle Ages, the saints were not merely dead persons but living presences in their lives, kept alive through the preaching of their priests, the art in their churches—statues, murals, and the like—and dramatized in pageants at religious festivals. The saints were woven through their lives, often local figures who were the subject of holy legends. In fact, the early saints (through much of the first millennium of the history of the Church) were just that: local Christians who had led exemplary lives or done some extraordinary good deeds, who were then proclaimed as saints upon their death.

ST. FRANCIS

St. Francis of Assisi (1181/82–1226) is another example of a transcendent saint, one of the most well-known and beloved of all the Christian saints of the canon. No doubt that's because his message of peace and love is simple and universal, touching the hearts of everyone who has read his Peace Prayer and who knows the stories of his life among the animals. His prayer is well-known among Catholics and others:

> *Lord make me an instrument of your peace.*
>
> *Where there is hatred,*
>
> *Let me sow love;*
>
> *Where there is injury, pardon;*
>
> *Where there is error, truth;*
>
> *Where there is doubt, faith;*
>
> *Where there is despair, hope;*
>
> *Where there is darkness, light;*
>
> *And where there is sadness, joy.*
>
> *O Divine Master grant that I may not so much seek to be*
>   *consoled*
>
> *As to console;*
>
> *To be understood, as to understand;*
>
> *To be loved, as to love.*
>
> *For it is in giving that we receive,*
>
> *It is in pardoning that we are pardoned,*
>
> *And it is in dying that we are born to eternal life.*

The image of St. Francis preaching to the birds with animals at his feet can be found in almost any nursery and garden store in America. This shows the message of St. Francis at its most commercial and its lowest common denominator, and the story of the saint is almost as simple—but not quite. When Francis began his holy life and was preaching his message of love to whoever would listen, it's recorded that he said he probably would have a better audience from the birds, and one day he tested that theory with this sermon:

"My brother birds, you should greatly praise your Creator and love Him always. He gave you feathers to wear, wings to fly, and whatever you need. God made you noble among his creatures and gave you a home in the purity of the air, so that, though you neither sow nor reap, He nevertheless protects and governs you without your least care."

Reports tell of a great multitude of birds—doves, crows, and magpies, among others—that listened to St. Francis and stayed with him as he spoke, allowing him to walk among them, touching and blessing them.

How did Francis come to walk among the animals and the poor, greeting everyone with the prayer "May the Lord give you peace"? Biographers tell us that, although his family was wealthy, Francis was born in a manger, his mother's way of paying homage to the birth of Jesus Christ. That act may have sown the seed for his life of devotion to God, but first Francis lived the life of a spoiled rich boy.

His father was a successful merchant dealing in lavish fabrics and materials, traveling far from home to acquire and trade his wares. Francis often accompanied him and had many worldly experiences, whereas most children his age at that time didn't venture far from their small villages. Francis' father was grooming him to take over the family business, but Francis had little interest in work and more in partying. He was generous with his father's money and shared it with his friends. In later years, Francis described his youth as a life of sin and debauchery.

It took mayhem, slaughter, and prison to completely change Francis. After his town of Assisi was attacked in the feudal wars, Francis survived, but at a terrible price. He was imprisoned in horrible conditions for a year until his father found him and paid a ransom for his release. Francis was then seriously ill and bedridden for another year, and although he wanted to join the Crusades and make something of his life, he could barely walk and had no strength for battle.

It was during this period that he had a spiritual awakening. A voice said to him, "Francis, don't you see that my house is being destroyed? Go then and rebuild it for me."

Francis took that as instructions from God to fix the dilapidated church outside his village, and he stole money from his father to do it. Although this was the beginning of his road to God, stealing was not a very saintly thing to do. It caused a permanent break with his father and Francis was now on his own, living in caves in the woods. He felt that he was an outcast and he decided that he wanted to share love and comfort with society's other outcasts, namely the lepers who suffered horribly. Francis could share only his comfort and love; he had nothing else to give them, but that, of course, was everything.

By reaching out to those less fortunate, to those who were hopeless, Francis was transformed—he finally understood God's calling. The message telling Francis to rebuild the church was a metaphor instructing him to rebuild the soul of the church, not the structure. The Lord made Francis an instrument of His peace and Francis not only attracted the birds and the beasts and the downtrodden, but one by one he built a band of brothers, friars who have grown into the Franciscan order. Today there are three main orders of the Franciscans and many thousands of monasteries and followers worldwide.

In 1224, two years before his death, Francis was on a retreat on Mount La Verna when he was marked with stigmata—the wounds of Christ's passion appeared on his hands, feet, and side. He died at the age of 45 and was canonized as a saint a mere two years later, one of the fastest canonizations since the process was centralized in the Vatican. We celebrate the feast day of St. Francis of Assisi on October 4, and there is a recently developed tradition in U.S. churches to offer the Blessing of the Animals on that day. It's a wonderful opportunity to travel to churches and see dogs, cats, horses, snakes, bunnies, and even goats sharing the church pews with their loving owners!

Additionally, Francis is one of the very few saints to have more than one feast day: September 17 used to be celebrated in the Universal Church as a secondary memorial of his receiving the stigmata. This feast was instituted after the Council of Trent in the late sixteenth century but suppressed by Pope Paul VI in 1969 (when the liturgical calendar was substantively revised and "cleaned up," removing such legendary saints as St. Christopher).

Francis' female counterpart and companion in faith, St. Clare of Assisi, is honored with her own memorial as well—earlier in the year on August 11, the day of her death in 1253. Clare followed her friend's example and founded a religious community of women devoted to the life of poverty. Although of noble birth herself, she walked barefoot in the same hills as St. Francis and led a group of sisters at San Damiano. The order she founded was named for her after her death: the Poor Clares. Among those who claim her as patron are goldsmiths, launderers, embroiderers, and needleworkers. (And television!)

ALL THE SAINTS

This brings us back to the post-Halloween period of November 1 and 2, which are commemorated as All Saints' Day and All Souls' Day, respectively. Remember that from the very first centuries and throughout the early Middle Ages, days were "assigned" to martyrs, sometimes (with the passage of time) to more than one. This became known as the "sanctoral cycle" or cycle of the holy men and women of the Church.

In this way, the Church exists in time—but outside or beyond the strictures of time—by reaching back to its origin and keeping alive the memory of the saints. One day in this never-ending cycle is set aside for special consideration to capture all those who have gone before who may or may not be given their own memorials and festivals as a kind of catch-all day on which to commemorate all saints whose names may have been lost through time.

In the United States it is a holy day of obligation (except, oddly, in the diocese of Honolulu, Hawaii), as well as in Chile, Honduras, Peru, and Puerto Rico. In Bolivia the observance is transferred to the first Sunday in November.

In this way, the season of autumn in the Northern Hemisphere, a time of harvest, is recognized as a divine harvest by God of all his good and faithful servants.

November opens a season of the year when our thoughts turn toward the fear of death, the hope of eternal life, the gratitude we feel for God's gifts, and the charity we owe to others. In the northern hemisphere, trees turn barren and the chill of late fall settles in to stay.

Laurence Hull Stookey devotes a chapter to the sanctoral cycle in his book *Calendar,* and points out that All Saints' Day emphasizes the unity of the Church across time. He quotes the redoubtable G. K. Chesterton, who, in the early twentieth century, wrote some profound works about Catholicism: "If you want to know the size of the Church, you have to count tombstones."

So yes, frankly, the Catholic Church is obsessed with death, as it is with sin and the weakness of human flesh. But the key to understanding the obsession is to focus on the transformative power of *resurrection,* as evidenced in the great Eastertide rising of Christ, then in the myriad resurrections of saints, which prefigure the resurrection of all at the end of days and for all eternity. Public festivals of the saints, as well as private devotions, ultimately are founded on that principle, and are thus an expression of that faith.

November 2 is set aside as the Commemoration of All the Faithful Departed, or All Souls' Day—which is a catchall of the catchall of the previous day: incorporating a remembrance of every single faithful Catholic or Christian who has passed, but who may or may not be recognized by the Church officially among the canon of the saints.

CHAPTER 14

THANKSGIVING AND CHRIST THE KING SUNDAY

The near-perfect melding of civic and religious purposes can be found in the celebration of Thanksgiving Day in the United States. It is not a Catholic holy day, per se.

The traditional story of the "first Thanksgiving" is compelling, as is the real history of the relations between the Pilgrims and the Native Americans of the 1620s. Over the next three centuries, this feast of harvest and friendship became the holiday we know today. In the Catholic tradition, the Protestant-originated holiday is acknowledged by the Church, usually with special readings and hymns in the daily Mass of the fourth Thursday of November. Often a parish church will consolidate its regular schedule of Masses (some have two or three a day) into a single Eucharistic celebration in mid-morning. That way the cooking and football-watching schedules are not disrupted.

For nearly 400 years, the familiar recounting of the first harvest feast in the Plymouth Colony has followed the same outline. About a year after their arduous voyage from England to escape religious strictures there, 202 members of the non-Anglican Christian sect who called themselves Pilgrims arrived in Massachusetts aboard the *Mayflower* in November 1620. After a devastating winter, they faced the spring season of sowing, in which they were aided by friendly Wampanoag Indians, Squanto and Samoset.

The subsequent harvest was bountiful. In November 1621, the 52 surviving colonists (of whom 28 were children) invited some 90 native people to share their feast in peace and friendship. It was seen as a model of how cooperation between the two cultures could actually be put into practice, though the comity between the settlers and the Indians in Massachusetts and elsewhere was short-lived.

Days of thanksgiving were not uncommon in Christian Europe prior to the Plymouth Colony's first feast. And earlier New World celebrations had been celebrated by Spanish and French explorers, as well as by previous English settlers in Maine and Jamestown, Virginia. But the Pilgrims' claim as the first Thanksgiving seemed to stick and became the conventional "first" in U.S. history.

One of the original Pilgrims, Edward Winslow, wrote how the celebration came about:

Our harvest being gotten in, our Governor sent four men on fowling, that so we might after a special manner rejoice together, after we had gathered the fruits of our labors; they four in one day killed as much fowl, as with a little help beside, served the company almost a week, at which time, amongst other recreations, we exercised our arms, many of the Indians coming amongst the rest their greatest king Massaoit, with some ninety men, whom for three days we entertained and feasted, and they went out and killed five deer, which they brought to the plantation and bestowed on our Governor, and upon the Captain and others. And although it be not always so plentiful, as it was at this time with us, yet by the goodness of God, we are so far from want, that we often wish you partakers of our plenty.

So the Pilgrims' festival was not one, but three days. Activities included games and dancing—and, as seen in the Winslow letter, shooting. The meals in all likelihood were eaten standing up during the festivities. The festival was a one-time event, not repeated the following year. Then, over time, Thanksgiving, modeled roughly on the Plymouth experience, became an official public holiday.

In September 1639, the legislature of Connecticut issued a Thanksgiving proclamation, which remained in effect for many years. In 1775, General George Washington directed his Continental troops to observe November 23 as Thanksgiving Day. The first Thanksgiving celebrated by all 13 colonies simultaneously was December 18, 1777, as determined by the Continental Congress.

As president of the new United States, Washington proclaimed November 26, 1789, as a day of thanksgiving for the newly adopted constitution. It wasn't until October 3, 1863, that President Abraham Lincoln declared the last Thursday in November as "an annual, general Thanksgiving day."

Nearly four score years later, in 1939, November had five Thursdays. Merchants believed that if there were more shopping days after Thanksgiving, sales would be greater. They asked President Franklin Roosevelt to change Thanksgiving from the last Thursday of November to the fourth Thursday. That year, Roosevelt complied, but 16 states balked, so 1939 became known as "the year of two thanksgivings." Congress then passed a law—after some further controversies over the "fourth" versus the "last" Friday—making the fourth Thursday of November the legal national holiday of Thanksgiving.

The Catholic bishops of the United States have approved a family prayer service around the Thanksgiving table, endorsing the public, civic celebration as consistent with the teaching of the Church. In addition to a candle-lighting and suggested cycle of petitions, this blessing is included:

Lord of all blessings,

from you has come a full harvest of gifts to us.

With our uplifted hearts,

we come today around this table

to give thanks to you.

We are grateful not only for the gifts of our very lives

but for all the gifts of friendship, love,

devotion and forgiveness that we have shared.

On this Thanksgiving and this day of giving thanks,

we thank you for showing us

how to return thanks by lives of service,

by actions of hospitality,

by kindness to others,

and by concern for each other.

[If guests are present:]

We thank you for the presence of [name guests],

who, by their being present in our home,

have added to this feast of joy and celebration.

We are most grateful, today,

for the way you, our unseen God, has become visible

to us in one another, both in our families and our friends

in countless daily gifts

and in the marvels of creation itself.

Come, Lord of Gifts,
bless our table and all the food of this feast.
Let us thank the Lord
today and all days.

Marking the end of November (the 30th day) and the end of Ordinary Time is the Memorial of St. Andrew, the first Apostle. Andrew is the patron saint of Scotland, as well as the patron of marriage and fertility, and is remembered from the Bible verse in which Jesus saw Andrew and his brother fishing in the Sea of Galilee and said, "Come follow me, and I will make you fishers of men" (Matthew 4:19).

Scots celebrate his feast day by baking scones with an X-shaped cross on top representing the type of cross on which St. Andrew was crucified. This shape was later used in the national flag and, blended with St. George's cross, the Union Jack, the flag of the United Kingdom. On the continent, German folk tradition, according to author Meredith Gould, has children going door to door to collect gifts or donations for charity for the feast of St. Andrew.

CHRIST THE KING

The days of celebration and memorial *always* come back to one thing and to one figure at the center of the Catholic faith: Christ. All festivals and holidays are, for the Church, ultimately about his redemption of the souls of believers. Holy days open the door between the earthly (and often earthy) life of us mortals and the divine: whether favorite saints, the Virgin Mary, or Jesus himself.

It is appropriate, then, that the final Sunday of Ordinary Time, in the last week before Advent and the beginning of the new liturgical year, is designated by the Catholic Church as the Solemnity of Our Lord Jesus Christ the King. This unique feast day focuses on the kingship or *authority* of Jesus Christ as teacher, ruler, and the one foretold as the Messiah or Anointed, the king of the Jews whom Herod the Great so feared.

Christ the King Sunday was formally moved from its centuries-old position on the final Sunday in October to its current spot as the final Sunday of Ordinary Time, immediately before the first Sunday of Advent, by Pope Pius XI in his 1925 encyclical *Quas Primas.* According to a Charles Irwin homily from Catholic Web, the early twentieth century was "a time when World War I had been fought, as well as a time when Communism, Nazism, and secularism were on the rise. . . . The popes in the 1800s and 1900s introduced other Church solemnities with similar origins. When reverence and devotion to the Blessed Sacrament had grown cold, the feast of Corpus Christi was instituted. So, too, the feast of the Sacred Heart of Jesus was instituted at a time when men and women were oppressed by the sad and gloomy severity of the Catholic version of Puritanism known as Jansenism."

In current usage and in today's secular society, the notion of "kingship" and the authority of kings seem, perhaps, antiquated. Yet the Church remains hierarchical in its structure, and especially in its divine origin and organization, with Christ as founder and head. And Scripture is replete with references to the kingship of Jesus of Nazareth, from the genealogy of the royal house of King David to the inscription upon the cross on which he died: *Iesus Nazarenus Rex Iudaeorum* (Jesus of Nazareth, King of the Jews). And there are telling New Testament passages:

> *[Jesus said,] "You know that those who are recognized as rulers over the Gentiles lord it over them, and their great ones make their authority over them felt. But it shall not be so among you. Rather, whoever wishes to become great among you will be your servant; whoever wishes to be first among you will be the slave of all. For the son of Man did not come to be served, but to serve, and to give his life as a ransom for many."*
>
> *—Mark 10:42–45*

> *Pilate said to Jesus, "Are you the king of the Jews?" . . . Jesus answered, "My kingdom does not belong to this world. If my kingdom did belong to this world, my attendants would be fighting to keep me from being handed over to the Jews. But as it is, my kingdom is not here." So Pilate said to him, "Then you are a king?" Jesus answered, "You say I am a king. For this I was born and for this I came into the world, to testify to the truth."*
>
> *—John 18:33, 36–37*

Pope Pius XI recognized that the Catholic Church was, in effect, bucking the prevailing mood of the world. It had long since moved through revolutions that had deposed kings, and the establishment of popular democracies, as well as brutal dictatorships—with more world-shattering events to come after Pius (who died in 1939) had passed from the scene.

But he had specific and very high hopes for the effect this solemnity might have. He wrote, "When once men recognize, both in private and in public life, that Christ is King, society will at last receive the great blessings of real liberty, well-ordered discipline, peace and harmony. Our Lord's regal office invests the human authority of princes and rulers with a religious significance; it ennobles the citizen's duty of obedience."

In fact, Pius hoped that this observance would encourage civic society to respect the freedom of the Church and its members and, as a result, give more respect to Christ through his people. He also prayed "that the faithful would gain strength and courage from the celebration of the feast, as we are reminded that Christ must reign in our hearts, minds, wills, and bodies." You can't blame a pope for hoping for the best, even against all odds.

Suffice it to say that the world has not accepted the "kingly authority" of Jesus of Nazareth, just as it did not in Christ's own time. After all, he was executed as a criminal by the people and the senate of Rome, through the state's representative, Pilate, and with the compliance of the Sanhedrin, which saw the young preacher as a rabble-rouser and blasphemer. There are no public holidays associated with this feast, which falls between two of the major annual holidays: Thanksgiving and Christmas.

The circle, then, is completed, from the opening of the liturgical year on the first Sunday of Advent until its conclusion in the week following Christ the King Sunday.

HOW THE SECOND VATICAN COUNCIL CHANGED THE CHURCH— AND ITS CALENDAR

P ope John XXIII shocked the world—and more important, his own cardinals—when he announced in 1959 that the bishops of the world would be summoned to the Vatican a few years afterward for an ecumenical council, the first in 92 years and only the second in 400 years.

John himself, beatified in 2000 (so that the title "Blessed" precedes his name), was beloved in his time by people around the world. He gave a new face to the Catholic Church after the severe and scholarly-looking Pius XII, who was the quintessential "insider" as a Roman-born pope and longtime member of the elite, bureaucratic Roman Curia. The peasant-born Good Pope John, as he was called, turned out to be a wily inside player himself and a master at public relations for the sake of his beloved Church.

Some of the hierarchy balked at the idea of a new council. The historical memory of the First Vatican Council (1869–70) was still on the minds of some of the older cardinals and bishops. That had been the council which defined "papal infallibility" and, for some, built up the walls around the Church against the modern world even higher. Many cardinals and bishops resisted change of any kind in the centuries-old rites and teachings of the Catholic Church, fearing that the structure could come tumbling down if the world was allowed into the incense-filled sacred precincts of the Vatican.

Nonetheless, Pope John got his way. After all, he was pope and the others were bound to obey their supreme pontiff (the old Roman term for high priest). With the help of Cardinal Montini, the archbishop of Milan and a favorite of the Good Pope, and other (primarily European) bishops, John XXIII saw that the debates on the floor of St. Peter's Basilica were opened up, in opposition to the wishes of Cardinals Siri and Ottaviani, for example, who represented the culturally and theologically ultra-conservative membership of the College of Bishops.

It was, in the end, a triumph for the progressive forces within the Church. Documents on liturgy, religious orders, the laity, and the relations of the Church with Jews and other non-Christians were passed and approved by the pope. John died on June 3, 1963.

The reformers won most of the battles and, indeed, the war, if that is how the council could be described, even if rather simplistically. In terms of the long history of the Church, the debates and the decisions by the council fathers were deemed momentous in their time—and seem so even today, two generations later. But it is also fair to say that the council's reforms caused no small amount of discomfort for some—in different ways in different parts of the world.

In response to the updating and opening actions of the council, Pope Paul VI—who had been elected between the first and second sessions of the council—promulgated a revision of the Roman Missal on April 3, 1969. What did this mean for Catholics in terms of practicing their faith and observing festivals, holy days, and saints' days?

Quite a bit, actually, just as the other changes instituted by the Second Vatican Council affected modes of worship and the role of the laity in the Church. In those days, Pope Paul was considered a leading reformer, one of the "good guys" in conflict with reactionary forces within the Church who would have preferred to close it off to the non-Catholic world and hang on to the Tridentine (or even pre-Council of Trent) norms of the "Church militant."

The chief instrument of the change was one of the first and most important documents produced by the council: the Constitution on the Sacred Liturgy, known by its Latin name, *Sacrosanctum Concilium* (from the first few words of the document, "This sacred Council"). It was approved nearly unanimously by a vote of 2,147 to 4, then signed as Church law and published by Pope Paul VI on December 4, 1963.

This sacred Council has several aims in view: It desires to impart an ever-increasing vigor to the Christian life of the faithful; to adapt more suitably to the needs of our own times those institutions which are subject to change; to foster what can promote union among all who believe in Christ; to strengthen whatever can help to call the whole of mankind into the household of the Church. The Council therefore sees particularly cogent reasons for undertaking the reform and promotion of the liturgy.

Quite an ambitious purpose! The real effects were profound.

This document was the first substantial reform of the rubrics (the prayers and outward movements) of the Mass, as well as the practice of the sacraments. The most visible and startling changes were to allow the Mass to be said in local languages, rather than Latin, and rearranging the altar so that the priest faced the people when celebrating Mass. Both changes were considered "revolutionary" at the time and required new translations and publications of Church materials, as well as a reorientation among Catholics everywhere.

The revision of the Roman Missal, the book that contains all the prayers and rites of the Church, was among the most important steps forward. Those who grew up as Catholics before the Second Vatican Council will remember taking their personal missals, smaller versions of the official book designed for the lay person, to and from Mass. It helped the people in the pews follow the liturgy on Sundays and saints' days and, in the United States, provided prayer texts in both Latin and English. Children's missals were given as First Communion gifts, and adult versions were given to Catholics on birthdays and other special occasions.

Dating to 1223, at the instigation of St. Francis of Assisi, the friars first adapted the Roman Missal for more general use, which eventually became the basis of a revised edition that became obligatory throughout the Church in 1570, during the prolonged period of the Council of Trent. Further corrections were made by popes for the next 450 years. Advances in printing technology made the missal available to more and more Catholics, especially in Europe and North America, so that it became the familiar link between the lay worshiper and the priest.

In the early twentieth century, the popes saw the need to make their own changes. Pius X famously encouraged more frequent reception of the Eucharist—on Sundays, feast days, and at daily Mass—and a younger age for first reception of Holy Communion. Pius XII instituted further changes in the missal that included the renewal of the promises of Baptism at the Easter Vigil, revision of the texts of Holy Week, and some changes in the calendar that affected the celebration of some feasts and saints' days.

So, after Vatican II had confirmed the need for further reforms and codified this in Church law, the pope gave his blessing to specific actions regarding the liturgical calendar.

Paul VI suppressed some 40 feast days, including some that were very popular, such as the feast of St. Christopher and the commemoration of St. Francis of Assisi's stigmata. In eliminating St. Christopher's feast day, the pope did not say that he was no longer a saint, but that is how the announcement was perceived by most, who were perhaps unaware of the theological subtleties of taking away the saint's "day."

One who came out ahead, so to speak, was St. Joseph, Jesus' earthly foster father. Joseph's name was inserted into the Eucharistic Prayer of the Mass, increasing his stature among the communion of saints and placing him closer to the Apostles and the Virgin Mary in the canon.

Pope Paul's purpose in implementing *Sacrosanctum Concilium*'s legislation regarding feasts and holy days was to put the emphasis back on the personal and soul-saving mission of Jesus Christ. Saints may come and go, important as they are. But, preeminent always, from the beginning to the end, is Jesus—on Sundays and other holy days dedicated to him:

> *The minds of the faithful must be directed primarily toward the feasts of the Lord whereby the mysteries of salvation are celebrated in the course of the year. Therefore, the proper of the time shall be*

given the preference which is due over the feasts of the saints, so that the entire cycle of the mysteries of salvation may be suitably recalled.

Second, though vitally important in the life of the Church, is Mary. She is, according to the *Sacrosanctum Concilium,* "joined by an inseparable bond to the saving work of her son. In her the Church holds up and admires the most excellent fruit of the redemption and joyfully contemplates, as in a faultless image, that which she herself desires and hopes wholly to be.

"The Church has also included in the annual cycle days devoted to the memory of the martyrs and other saints. Raised up to perfection by the manifold grace of God, and already in possession of eternal salvation, they sing God's perfect praise in heaven and offer prayers for us."

Further, Pope Paul wished to fulfill the council's purpose of modernizing the outward practices of the Church without disturbing the foundational dogmatic teachings of the faith. Again, it was clear that certain less familiar saints and other auxiliary devotions such as the Sacred Heart or minor local traditions (known as "cultus") that could tie some of the pious faithful in spiritual knots could be jettisoned.

Always hierarchical in structure and based in Hebrew monotheism with philosophical pillars borrowed from the Greeks to help support the edifice, the Catholic Church could, as it had throughout history, revise its calendar and require the faithful to learn new ways to express their ancient faith.

AFTERWORD

One of the most haunting poems in the English language in my opinion, ranking with Poe's gloomy *Raven*, is *The Hound of Heaven* by Francis Thompson. Arguably a minor poem in the grand scheme of things, and composed by a distinctly minor poet, it still looms large in the Catholic imagination some hundred years after the author's death, as it paints an emotionally charged picture of the irresistible power of God, of good, and of the Church.

At first, the hapless narrator of *Hound* resists with all his might:

> *I fled Him, down the nights and down the days;*
> *I fled Him, down the arches of the years;*
> *I fled Him, down the labyrinthine ways*
> *Of my own mind; and in the midst of tears*
> *I hid from him, and under running laughter.*

But inexorably, over time, through dreams and denial, the Hound—who is God himself—catches the fleeing sinner,

the wretched weakling, and will not let him go. He speaks to
his prey:

> *"How little worthy of any love thou art!*
> *Whom wilt thou find to love ignoble thee,*
> *Save Me, save only Me?*
> *All which I took from thee I did but take,*
> *Not for thy harms,*
> *But just that though might'st seek it in My arms.*
> *All which thy child's mistake*
> *Fancies as lost, I have stored for thee at home:*
> *Rise, clasp My hand, and come!"*

Overcoming distance and all resistance, the ultimate
power wins over the human being who is frightened of his
own good and of God's best intentions for him. Significantly,
the divine love overcomes the "days" and the "years" that
man throws up as barriers between himself and God's will
for him. The point of Thompson's poem is that such defenses
cannot and will not ever work for such a purpose.

Indeed, the Catholic point of view is that time is a gift
of the Creator to the created. Time, like other physical and
spiritual gifts, is a beautiful, intricate, and intimate opportunity—not an enemy to be fought or an obstacle to be
overcome.

The Church's message to the believer, then, is: "Go with
the flow."

As we have seen throughout the course of this book, that "flow" has existed, for Christians, for the past two thousand years. For those same believers, it will continue until the end times, otherwise known as the Day of Judgment— perhaps the biggest and baddest "holy day of obligation" of all! For we will all be obliged to be present to face our Maker on that day.

In the meantime, from sunrise to sunset on each day we have been given, the "flow" continues unabated. Therefore, it behooves us to mark the time and to spend the time mindful of its origin and its ultimate destination—and *our* origin and *our* ultimate destination.

The footsteps the fleeing wretch of *The Hound of Heaven* hears behind him continue the "unhurrying chase" at an "unperturbed pace," with "deliberate speed" and "majestic instancy." The beat, as in a musical number or as in the human heart, is unstoppable. The rhythm continues in "morning's eyes" as well as in "the red throb" of sunset, through "the pillaring hours" and upon "the mounded years."

All day. Every day. For all eternity. With all deliberate speed and majestic instancy.

As we have seen, Catholic Church festivals reached their highest expression and deepest penetration of the human soul during the Middle Ages. From the so-called barbarian conversions of northern Europe around A.D. 1000 and for another five hundred years until Martin Luther sparked the Protestant Reformation, the Church held sway over the hearts and minds of Christendom. The mystery of the liturgy and the majesty of divinely sanctioned kings seemed irrevocable facts of life for the masses—never to be challenged or changed by mere men.

During this period, the Church also established the university system in populous cities such as Paris and Bologna, which quickly brought scholarship and the idea of higher learning to a new level that would infuse all of Western civilization with Catholic intellectual principals. Some of these principles trickled down to the people, and some did not trickle up to the powers that occupied the papal throne (think of Galileo and Copernicus).

For the regular people, their days, seasons, and years were scored with holy festivals that interrupted time and allowed them some rest and recreation from tending their fields or plying their trades. Such festivals opened heaven to the common people, giving them a glimpse of the afterlife, of paradise, of saints and angels.

Being human, fears and superstitions sometimes overrode the more sublime purposes of priests, bishops, and popes. And, over the past 500 years, when the Western world passed through the Renaissance and the Enlightenment, the hold of religion on the masses has steadily declined. Today, according to surveys and polls, the United

States is probably the most religious country in the West, with "Old Europe" having fallen away from Christian observance further and faster since World War II than at any other period in the last two millennia.

Yet Christmas, Easter, and local and national saints' days remain embedded in the consciousness of the once-Christian and once-dominant civilization that had sprung into lush flower from the deep roots of Rome and Greece. What American child does not know about Valentine's Day cards and candies or Halloween costumes and trick-or-treating? What Mexican child has not seen the image of Our Lady of Guadalupe countless times—on posters and religious medals, in secular and church settings alike?

Our world is now hundreds of generations removed from the first Pentecost and the first stirrings of the Jesus movement that became the Christian Church. Ours is a time of secularization, religious debate, a new rise in the scope and influence of Islam (now the largest single religion in the world, with about 1.3 billion adherents, with Catholicism in second place at 1.2 billion). Much has changed, of course. But much remains the same.

Although our work week is now generally five days of 35 to 40 hours, we still crave weekends and holidays for relaxation and "family time." Far fewer attend Sunday Mass today than at any other time since the 1950s, and there are far fewer women entering religious orders as nuns. Everyone knows that the numbing parade of scandalous revelations in the early years of this century has taken a deadly toll on the Church's moral reputation and credibility. But the decline in numbers of qualified men entering the Catholic priesthood has bottomed out and is even increasing in some areas—especially former missionary countries in Africa and Asia—and hundreds of thousands of adults are entering the Church as converts every year.

Something is happening out there, and it is not all bad news for Catholics and their Church—for those who hold to the belief in the forgiveness of sins, the communion of saints, and the resurrection of the dead.

In our everyday lives, the great traditions of the Church survive in manners, food, and words—and also in the ways in which we mark time and celebrate our humanity. If nothing else, the Catholic Church lives up to its name, meaning "universal." It is a binding agent, a kind of spiritual glue, that still holds us together in communities large and small. An Irish American from Philadelphia would not be out of place at an Easter celebration in Manila, the Philippines, though many of the foods and customs would seem quite exotic—while being quite Catholic, too.

In exploring the meanings of holy days as defined by the Catholic tradition and holidays as experienced by all of us, Catholic and non-Catholic alike, I have come to appreciate the sacred in every day. I now better understand how and why Sunday is the important day it is: the "eighth" day, the first day of the week, the day of high Masses and Super

Bowls. Each purpose for which a day might be set apart has some spiritual significance, even if tenuously (I'll leave it to someone else to argue for the spirituality of the NFL).

Thus, each day, whether it is devoted to a certain saint or the occasion for a parade or barbecue, is invested with possibility. Each morning with hope. Each noon with the sun's brightness or a high point in one's activity. Each evening with a bit of sadness at the day's final passing into night.

The cycle of our lives and our rituals and observances, religious or secular, helps not only to mark the time but to define us. We are what we choose to be. We are what we choose to do. We are what we choose to believe—about one another and about a power up there, out there, or in here that is greater than our own egos. We are what we seek: purpose beyond the present moment or the present task. Each little *thing*, such as a Christmas stocking or a firecracker, may mean a lot in the moment and so often represents a lot more in the "bigger picture."

Time, seen through the Catholic lens, is an instrument of salvation, the hours devoted to prayer, the days to memory, the weeks, months, and seasons to concepts beyond our human imagining—that is, if we choose to approach time with a bit of faith and hope in our hearts. And perhaps a bit of charity, of love for family and neighbor, a willingness to be a part, with them, of a greater world for a greater purpose.

Was Jesus really born on Christmas? In *my* heart he certainly was. Or, to flip the coin: Was Christmas really born with Jesus? Certainly we know this is true. Although we may try to amend or even warp the concept of the holy day, the origin of the idea lies in the spirit, however true or false any historical claim may prove to be.

May your Christmases, Easters, Halloweens, and St. Patrick's Days, *ad infinitum*—and even Super Bowl Sundays!—from now on be filled with genuine celebration and joy that contain a glimpse of the divine that we human beings have sought for so long—indeed, forever.

APPENDIX A

SACROSANCTUM CONCILIUM

CONSTITUTION ON THE SACRED LITURGY

SACROSANCTUM CONCILIUM

SOLEMNLY PROMULGATED BY

HIS HOLINESS, POPE PAUL VI

ON DECEMBER 4, 1963

Sections 102–111 from Chapter V: The Liturgical Year, within the document

102   Holy Mother Church is conscious that she must celebrate the saving work of her divine Spouse by devoutly recalling it on certain days throughout the course of the year. Every week, on the day which she has called the Lord's Day, she keeps the memory of the Lord's resurrection, which she also celebrates once in the year, together with His blessed passion, in the most solemn festival of Easter.

Within the cycle of a year, moreover, she unfolds the whole mystery of Christ, from the incarnation and birth until the ascension, the day of Pentecost, and the expectation of blessed hope and of the coming of the Lord.

Recalling thus the mysteries of redemption, the Church opens to the faithful the riches of her Lord's powers and merits, so that these are in some way made present for all time, and the faithful are enabled to lay hold upon them and become filled with saving grace.

103   In celebrating this annual cycle of Christ's mysteries, holy Church honors with especial love the Blessed Mary, Mother of God, who is joined by an inseparable bond to the saving work of her Son. In her the Church holds up and admires the most excellent fruit of the redemption, and joyfully contemplates, as in a faultless image that which she herself desires and hopes wholly to be.

104   The Church has also included in the annual cycle days devoted to the memory of the martyrs and other saints. Raised up to perfection by the manifold grace of God, and already in possession of eternal salvation, they sing God's perfect praise in heaven and offer prayers for us. By celebrating the passage of these saints from earth to heaven the Church proclaims the paschal mystery achieved in the saints who have suffered and been glorified with Christ, she proposes them to the faithful as examples drawing all to the Father through Christ, and through their merits she pleads for God's favors.

105   Finally, in the various seasons of the year and according other traditional discipline, the Church completes the formation of the faithful by means of pious practices for soul and body, by instruction, prayer, and works of penance and mercy.

Accordingly the sacred Council has seen fit to decree as follows.

106   By a tradition handed down from the Apostles which took its origin from the very day of Christ's resurrection, the Church celebrates the paschal mystery every eighth day, with good reason this, then, bears the name of the Lord's Day or Sunday. For on this day Christ's faithful are bound to come together into one place so that, by hearing the word of God and taking part in the Eucharist, they may call to mind the passion, the resurrection and the glorification of the Lord Jesus, and may thank God who "has begotten them again, through the resurrection of Jesus Christ from the dead, unto a living hope" (1 Peter 1:3). Hence the Lord's day is the original feast day, and it should be proposed to the piety of the faithful and taught to them so that it may be-

come in fact a day of joy and of freedom from work. Other celebrations, unless they be truly of greatest importance, shall not have precedence over the Sunday which is the foundation and kernel of the whole liturgical year.

107   The liturgical year is to be revised so that the traditional customs and discipline of the sacred seasons shall be preserved or restored to suit the conditions of modern times; their specific character is to be retained, so that they duly nourish the piety of the faithful who celebrate the mysteries of Christian redemption, and above all the paschal mystery. If certain adaptations are considered necessary on account of local conditions, they are to be made in accordance with the provisions of Articles 39 and 40.

108   The minds of the faithful must be directed primarily toward the feasts of the Lord whereby the mysteries of salvation are celebrated in the course of the year. Therefore, the proper of the time shall be given the preference which is its due over the feasts of the saints, so that the entire cycle of the mysteries of salvation may be suitably recalled.

109   The season of Lent has a twofold character: primarily by recalling or preparing for baptism and by penance, it disposes the faithful, who more diligently hear the word of God and devote themselves to prayer, to celebrate the paschal mystery. This twofold character is to be brought into greater prominence both in the liturgy and by liturgical catechesis. Hence:

(a) More use is to be made of the baptismal features proper to the Lenten liturgy, some of them, which used to flourish in bygone days, are to be restored as may seem good.

(b) The same is to apply to the penitential elements. As regards instruction it is important to impress on the minds of the faithful not only the social consequences of sin but also that essence of the virtue of penance which leads to the detestation of sin as an offence against God; the role of the Church in penitential practices is not to be passed over, and the people must be exhorted to pray for sinners.

110   During Lent penance should not be only internal and individual, but also external and social. The practice of penance should be fostered in ways that are possible in our own times and in different regions, and according to the circumstances of the faith-

ful; it should be encouraged by the authorities mentioned in Article 22.

Nevertheless, let the paschal fast be kept sacred. Let it be celebrated everywhere on Good Friday and, where possible, prolonged throughout Holy Saturday, so that the joys of the Sunday of the resurrection may be attained with uplifted and clear mind.

111 The saints have been traditionally honored in the Church and their authentic relics and images held in veneration. For the feasts of the saints proclaim the wonderful works of Christ in His servants, and display to the faithful fitting examples for their imitation.

Lest the feasts of the saints should take precedence over the feasts which commemorate the very mysteries of salvation, many of them should be left to be celebrated by a particular Church or nation or family of religious; only those should be extended to the universal Church which commemorate saints who are truly of universal importance.

APPENDIX B

PATRON SAINTS AROUND THE WORLD

If all politics is local, the same might be said for saints. We owe the notion of patron saints to early witnesses for Christ who gave their lives defending the faith or otherwise living exemplary Christ-centered lives—and making particular contributions in the world, for which they are fondly remembered. Well before the Church established a formal structure for beatification and canonization, local heroes were remembered at grave sites and cemeteries.

Over time, the fame of these local martyrs and witnesses spread beyond their home regions. As someone once put it, "All saints were patrons."

In modern terms, you could think of patron saints as being in-house advocates, spiritual lobbyists, champions, or coaches. They are akin to the list of patrons of the arts you see when you attend a local play, opera, or ballet. Instead of these patrons being financial donors, they press our case to the heavens. And in the case of patrons of countries, they do so on a communal level.

To those who object, "Who needs saints as intercessors? I go straight to God—to Jesus Christ," I say, point taken.

But patron saints are intercessors, not mediators (a subtle, but important, distinction). From a human and ancient perspective, it is only natural for us to turn to heroes to unite us in prayer. After all, we do this all the time on a purely secular level. Every country has founding fathers and mothers who are revered by the populace and honored on special days we call holidays.

By way of mild digression, let me say that the bundling of holidays to accommodate long weekends divorces us from the importance of the day itself. The holiday should mark an occasion that honors the person or the event on its own merits, not as a means to some end, such as recreation or respite. In other words, save that stuff for bank holidays, as in Europe; keep the day sacred for the person being remembered.

When it comes to patron saints around the world, we often remember the day he or she died, or, in other words, their Christian day of "birth into a new life." The feast might celebrate a particular event in Church or national history or a purported local miracle.

In some countries, the patron saint's feast day is still celebrated as a secular holiday, even in countries that otherwise seem to lack devotion and religiosity. For one day (more than one day, if several patronal feast days are observed), we find a marriage of the sacred and the profane, of the religious and the secular.

Thus, in the Czech Republic, September 28 marks the feast of St. Wenceslaus as well as national statehood. In Ireland too (and for people of Irish descent worldwide), St. Patrick's Day, March 17, offers a chance to identify with the saint who endured slavery, taught the Trinity, and became (perhaps despite himself) a nation-making figure. Mexicans, and Catholics throughout North America, celebrate a similar unifying force under the banner of Our Lady of Guadalupe, on December 12.

Whether in times of peril, great need, or thanksgiving, peoples of nations—believers and nonbelievers alike—have gravitated to their patron saints for strength and spiritual connection.

The list provided here is neither exhaustive nor encyclopedic. There is no official Spiritual Hall of Fame. The cataloguing of patron saints employs a mix of official Church declarations, local custom, tradition, and folklore—elements that change and grow, or wane, over the years.

NORTH AMERICAN SAINTS

According to the national calendar of the United States, as requested by the United States Conference of Catholic Bishops (USCCB) and approved by the Holy See:

January 4	Saint Elizabeth Ann Seton, religious—Memorial
January 5	Saint John Neumann, bishop—Memorial
January 6	Saint André Bessette, religious—Optional Memorial
March 3	Saint Katharine Drexel, virgin—Optional Memorial
May 10	Saint Damien Joseph de Veuster of Moloka'i, priest—Optional Memorial
May 15	Saint Isidore (the Farmer)—Optional Memorial
July 1	Blessed Junípero Serra, priest—Optional Memorial
July 14	Blessed Kateri Tekakwitha, virgin—Memorial
July 18	Saint Camillus de Lellis, priest—Optional Memorial

August 18	Saint Jane Frances de Chantal, religious—Optional Memorial
September 9	Saint Peter Claver, priest—Memorial
October 6	Blessed Marie-Rose Durocher, virgin—Optional Memorial
October 19	Saints John de Brébeuf and Isaac Jogues, priests and martyrs, and their companions, martyrs—Memorial
October 20	Saint Paul of the Cross, priest—Optional Memorial
November 13	Saint Frances Xavier Cabrini, virgin—Memorial
November 18	Saint Rose Philippine Duchesne, virgin—Optional Memorial
November 23	Blessed Miguel Agustín Pro, priest and martyr—Optional Memorial
December 12	Our Lady of Guadalupe—Feast

According to the national calendar of Canada, as requested by the Canadian Conference of Catholic Bishops (CCCB) and approved by the Holy See:

January 4	Saint Elizabeth Ann Seton (Archdiocese of Halifax)—Memorial
January 6	Saint Andre Bessette—Optional Memorial
January 12	Saint Marguerite Bourgeoys—Memorial
March 19	Saint Joseph, Patron of Canada—Solemnity
April 18	Blessed Marie-Anne Blodin—Optional Memorial
April 26	Our Lady of Good Counsel (Catholic Women's League)—Optional Memorial
April 30	Blessed Marie of the Incarnation—Optional Memorial
May 4	Blessed Marie-Leonie Paradis—Optional Memorial

May 6	Blessed Francois de Laval—Optional Memorial
May 8	Blessed Catherine of Saint Augustine—Optional Memorial
May 21	Saint Eugene de Mazenod—Optional Memorial
May 24	Blessed Louis-Zephirin Moreau—Optional Memorial
July 14	Blessed Kateri Tekakwitha—Optional Memorial
July 26	Saints Anne and Joachim, parents of Mary—Feast
August 5	Blessed Frederic Janssoone—Optional Memorial
September 4	Blessed Dina Belanger—Optional Memorial
September 23	Blessed Emilie Tavernier-Gamelin—Optional Memorial
September 26	Saints John de Brebeuf, Isaac Jogues and Companions—Feast
October 6	Blessed Marie-Rose Durocher—Optional Memorial
October 16	Saint Marie-Marguerite d'Youville—Memorial
December 12	Our Lady of Guadalupe—Feast

ACKNOWLEDGMENTS

First and foremost, I must acknowledge and thank Michael P. Foley, author of *Why Do Catholics Eat Fish on Friday?* That book opened the door wide for readers around the world, all of whom were happy to walk through it to discover fun and often hidden Catholic meanings and origins to "just about everything."

My publisher, Palgrave Macmillan, sought out this book and has supported it in extraordinary ways. Executive Editor Alessandra Bastagli and Senior Editor Colleen Lawrie put me on the path—and helped me to stay there. Colleen's deft editorial pen (or cursor, as the case may be) kept the words in proper order and the author focused. Cynthia Rodriguez, the proofreader, contended with some knotty sentences and questionable facts.

My longtime friend and colleague, freelancer Paul Kocak, walked with me on this journey. His research, fact-checking, editing skills and great ideas made the manuscript whole and complete, and so much better than if I had not asked him to help me. I also asked Kate Hartson and Patrick Justin Fahey for some last-minute help with research on particular topics, and they came through, adding much in little time.

Rev. Stephen Fichter encouraged me to mine the riches of the Second Vatican Council to illuminate the themes of the book. Seton Hall University colleagues, and my family, offered enthusiastic support as well. Rev. Paul Holmes kindly proofread and corrected the text significantly. Rev. Michael Walters also carefully proofread these pages and was equally generous with wise corrections.

The venerable Frank Weimann of the Literary Group International and his dynamic associate, Elyse Tanzillo, made this book a possibility for me and ensured that it became a reality. They have my special gratitude.

BIBLIOGRAPHY

BOOKS AND ARTICLES

Aveni, Anthony F., *The Book of the Year: A Brief History of Our Seasonal Holidays.* New York: Oxford University Press, 2003.

Catechism of the Catholic Church. New York: Doubleday, 1995.

Christianson, Stephen G., ed., *The American Book of Days.* New York: H. W. Wilson Co., 2000.

Coleman, Penny, *Thanksgiving: The True Story.* New York: Henry Holt, 2008.

Delaney, John J., *Lives of the Saints.* New York: Doubleday, 1980.

Doherty, Brian, *This Is Burning Man: The Rise of a New American Underground.* Dallas: BenBella Books, 2004.

Duncan, David Ewing, *Calendar: Humanity's Epic Struggle to Determine a True and Accurate Year.* New York: Avon Books, 1998.

Ehrenreich, Barbara, *Dancing in the Streets: A History of Collective Joy.* New York: Metropolitan Books, 2006.

Eliot, Jock, *Inventing Christmas: How Our Holiday Came to Be.* New York: Harry N. Abrams, Inc., 2001.

Farmer, David Hugh, *The Oxford Dictionary of Saints.* New York: Oxford University Press, 2004.

Foley, Michael P., *Why Do Catholics Eat Fish on Friday? The Catholic Origin to Just About Everything.* New York: Palgrave Macmillan, 2005.

Ganssle, Gregory E. and David M. Woodruff, eds., *God and Time: Essays on the Divine Nature.* New York: Oxford University Press, 2002.

Gould, Meredith, *The Catholic Home: Celebrations and Traditions for Holidays, Feast Days, and Every Day.* New York: Doubleday, 2004.

Hazleton, Lesley, *Mary: A Flesh-and-Blood Biography of the Virgin Mother.* New York: Bloomsbury Press, 2004.

Helfman, Elizabeth S., *Celebrating Nature.* New York: Seabury Press, 1969.

Heschel, Abraham Joshua, *The Sabbath: Its Meaning for Modern Man.* New York: Farrar, Straus and Giroux, 1979.

Hess, Debra, *The Fourth of July.* Tarrytown, NY: Benchmark Books/Marshall Cavendish, 2004.

Kelly, J. N. D., *The Oxford Dictionary of Popes.* New York: Oxford University Press, 1996.

Krythe, Maymie. R., *All About American Holidays.* New York: Harper and Row, 1962.

Liturgical Training Publications, *Liturgical Calendar 2010.* Chicago: LTP, 2009.

McBrien, Richard P., *Lives of the Saints.* San Francisco: HarperOne, 2001.

Moynahan, Brian, *The Faith: A History of Christianity.* New York: Doubleday, 2002.

Neville, Robert Cummings, *Eternity and Time's Flow.* Albany: State University of New York Press, 1993.

Richards, E. G., *Mapping Time: The Calendar and Its History.* New York: Oxford University Press, 1998.

Skal, David J., *Death Makes a Holiday: A Cultural History of Halloween.* New York: Bloomsbury Press, 2002.

Spoto, Donald, *Relucant Saint: Francis of Assisi.* New York: Viking Books, 2002.

Steel, Duncan, *Marking Time: The Epic Quest to Invent the Perfect Calendar.* New York: John Wiley & Sons, 2000.

Stookey, Laurence Hull, *Calendar: Christ's Time for the Church.* Nashville: Abingdon Press, 1996.

Thompson, Sue Ellen, *Holiday Symbols and Customs.* Detroit: Omnigraphics, 2003.

Turner, Paul, *Sourcebook for Sundays and Seasons: An Almanac of Parish Liturgy.* Chicago: LTP, 2005.

Urdang, Laurence and Christine N. Donohue, eds., *Holidays and Anniversaries of the World.* Detroit: Gale Research Company, 1985.

WEBSITES

www.americancatholic.org
www.marylinks.org
www.newadvent.org/catholicencyclopedia/cathen/
www.npr.org
www.ny-archdiocese.org
www.plimoth.org
www.usccb.org
www.usflag.org
www.vatican.va

INDEX